Prague

DIRECTIONS

WRITTEN AND RESEARCHED BY

Rob Humphreys

ROUGH GUIDES

NEW YORK • LONDON • DELHI

www.roughguides.com

Contents

Introduction to

Prague

Most people come to Prague because they've heard it's a beautiful place, and they're rarely disappointed. With some six hundred years of architecture virtually untouched by natural disaster or war, few other European capitals look as good. The city retains much of its medieval layout and its rich mantle of Baroque, Rococo and Art Nouveau buildings have successfully escaped the vanities and excesses of post-war redevelopment.

Physically, Prague may have weathered the twentieth century very well but it suffered in other ways. The city that produced the music of Dvořák and Smetana, the literature of Čapek and Kafka and modernist architecture to rival Bauhaus, was forced to endure a brutal Nazi occupation. Then for forty years, during the Communist period, the city lay hidden behind the Iron Curtain, seldom visited by Westerners. All that changed in the 1990s and nowadays, Prague is one of the most popular European city break destinations,

When to visit

Prague is now so popular that the streets around the main sights are jam-packed with tourists for much of the year. If you can, it's best to avoid the summer months, when temperatures soar above 30°C, and you have to fight your way across the Charles Bridge. The best times to visit, in terms of weather, are May and September. The winter months can be very chilly in Prague, but if you don't mind the cold, the city does look good in the snow and the crowds are manageable. Christmas and New Year are perfect: there are Christmas markets right across town, and plenty of mulled wine and hot punch to keep you warm.

▲ Malá Strana

with a highly developed tourist industry and a large expat population who, if nothing else, help to boost the city's nightlife.

The River Vltava winds its way through the heart of Prague, providing the city with its most enduring landmark, the Charles Bridge. Built during the city's medieval golden age, this stone bridge, with its parade of Baroque statuary, still forms the chief link between the old town and Prague's hilltop castle. The city is surprisingly compact, making it a great place to explore on foot, and despite the twisting matrix of streets, it's easy enough to find your way around between the major landmarks. If you do use public transport, you'll find a pic-

▼ Charles Bridge

turesque tram network and a futuristic Soviet-built metro system that rivals most German cities. And, for the moment at least, it's still a potentially inexpensive destination, with food and perhaps, most famously beer, costing below the EU average.

▲ Prague Castle

Prague
AT A GLANCE

PRAGUE CASTLE

The city's left bank is dominated by Prague Castle or Hrad, which contains the city's cathedral, the old royal palace and gardens, and a host of museums and galleries.

▲ Prague Cathedral

HRADČANY

The district immediately outside the castle gates is a wonderfully quiet quarter filled with old palaces housing government ministries and embassies.

MALÁ STRANA

Squeezed between Prague Castle and the river is the picturesque district of Malá Strana, with its twisting cobbled streets, Baroque palaces and secret walled gardens.

▼ Staré Město

STARÉ MĚSTO

The medieval hub of the city, Staré Město – literally, the "Old Town" – is probably the most visited part of the city, and has a huge number of pubs, bars and restaurants packed into its labyrinthine layout.

JOSEFOV

Enclosed within the boundaries of Staré Město is the former Jewish quarter, Josefov. The ghetto walls

▼ Josefov

▲ Wenceslas Square

have long since gone and the whole area was remodelled at the end of the nineteenth century, but six synagogues, a medieval cemetery and a town hall survive as powerful reminders of a community that has existed here for over a millennium.

WENCESLAS SQUARE

More of a wide boulevard than a square, it was here that Czechs gathered in their thousands during the 1989 Velvet Revolution.

▲ Nové Město

NOVÉ MĚSTO

Nové Město, the city's commercial and business centre, is a large sprawling district that fans out from Wenceslas Square (Václavské náměstí), focus of the political upheavals of the modern-day republic.

VYŠEHRAD, VINOHRADY AND ŽIŽKOV

The fortress of Vyšehrad was one of the earliest points of settlement in Prague, whereas Vinohrady & Žižkov are rather grand late-nineteenth-century suburbs.

▼ Vinohrady

HOLEŠOVICE

Another late nineteenth-century development, Holešovice is home to Prague's impressive museum of modern art, the Veletržní Palace, and Výstaviště, its old-fashioned trade fair grounds.

Ideas

The big six

You can have a great time in Prague just wandering the streets and wondering at the architecture, but there are six big sights you should definitely make the effort to see, no matter how short your visit. Few people miss Prague's medieval Charles Bridge and the picturesque Old Town Square, but it's also worth exploring Prague Castle, home to the city's cathedral, old royal palace and gardens; Josefov, Prague's former Jewish ghetto; the Art Nouveau Obecní dům; and Wenceslas Square, where the 1989 Velvet Revolution took place.

▲ **Prague Castle**

Towering over the city, the castle is the ultimate picture-postcard image of Prague.

P.49 ▶ PRAGUE CASTLE

▲ **Obecní dům**

Café, bar, restaurant, exhibition space and concert hall, this Art Nouveau masterpiece is preserved exactly as built in 1911.

P.98 ▶ WENCESLAS SQUARE AND NORTHERN NOVÉ MĚSTO

▲ Wenceslas Square

The modern hub of Prague, this sloping boulevard was the scene of the 1989 Velvet Revolution.

P.95 › WENCESLAS SQUARE AND NORTHERN NOVÉ MĚSTO

▼ Charles Bridge

Decorated with extravagant ecclesiastical statues, this medieval stone bridge is the city's most enduring monument.

P.72 › STARÉ MĚSTO

▲ Old Town Square

The city's showpiece square, lined with exquisite Baroque facades and overlooked by the town hall's famous astronomical clock.

P.76 › STARÉ MĚSTO

▼ Josefov

The former Jewish ghetto contains no fewer than six synagogues, a town hall and a remarkable medieval cemetery.

P.88 › JOSEFOV

Hotels

The food and drink may be cheap, but Prague is no budget destination when it comes to hotels. However, with so many ancient buildings to choose from, and more competition than ever among hoteliers, the city now has a good selection of places to stay, many of which have real character.

▼ Dum U velké boty

For attentive service and stylish antique decor, head for this discreet bolthole in the backstreets of Malá Strana.

P.134 ▸ MALÁ STRANA

▼ Černý slon

Simple rooms tucked away down an alleyway off the Old Town Square itself.

P.135 ▸ STARÉ MĚSTO

▲ Cloister Inn

A former nunnery hidden in the backstreets of Staré Město.

P.135 ▶ STARÉ MĚSTO

▲ U červeného lva

A classic Prague hotel with original seventeenth-century wooden ceilings and tasteful antique furnishings, including rugs over parquet flooring.

P.134 ▶ MALÁ STRANA

▼ U medvídků

If you're looking for unpretentious, inexpensive and centrally located rooms, try one of Prague's most authentic pubs.

P.137 ▶ MALÁ STRANA

▼ Josef

Prague's leading designer hotel is a minimalist symphony of off-white efficiency.

P.135 ▶ NOVÉ MĚSTO

Green Prague

Prague doesn't have a vast number of parks, but it does have a whole host of wonderful hidden Baroque gardens in Malá Strana, several of which are linked via terraces to the gardens around the castle. The largest green space in the centre is the Petřín hill, accessible via a funicular railway, and boasting great views over the city. Further afield, Vyšehrad's fortress and the woods of Stromovka are good places to lose the crowds in summer.

▲ Kampa

The chief park on the island of Kampa enjoys fine views across to Staré Město.

P.66 ▶ MALÁ STRANA

▲ Malá Strana terraced gardens

Pretty little Baroque gardens laid out on the terraced slopes below the castle.

P.OOO ▶ MALÁ STRANA

▲ Vyšehrad

This old Habsburg military fortress is now a great escape from the busy city.

P.113 ▶ VYŠEHRAD, VINOHRADY AND ŽIŽKOV

◀ Stromovka

Large leafy park laid out between Výstaviště and the chateau of Troja.

P.126 ▶ HOLEŠOVICE

▶ Petřín

This wooded hill on Prague's left bank provides a spectacular viewpoint over the city.

P.68 ▶ MALÁ STRANA

▼ Royal Gardens

Castle gardens famous for their disciplined crops of tulips.

P.57 ▶ PRAGUE CASTLE

Baroque Prague

The full force of the Counter-Reformation was brought to bear on the Czechs, who took to Protestantism en masse in the Renaissance period. The legacy of this ideological battle can be seen in the city's enormous wealth of Baroque art and architecture: great Italianate domes dominate the skyline and melodramatic statuary peppers the streets – most famously, the Charles Bridge.

▼ Cathedral of sv Vít

The Tomb of St John of Nepomuk in the city's cathedral is the most spectacular reminder of the former power of the Jesuits.

P.49 › PRAGUE CASTLE

▼ Old Town Square

Probably the most impressive parade of Baroque facades and gables in all Prague.

P.76 › STARÉ MĚSTO

▶ Charles Bridge statues

It's the (mostly) Baroque statues that make this medieval bridge so unforgettable.

P.72 ▸ STARÉ MĚSTO

◀ Klementinum

The Jesuits' former powerhouse still retains several Baroque masterpieces from the time.

P.73 ▸ STARÉ MĚSTO

◀ Loreto church

A sumptuous Baroque pilgrimage complex with frescoed cloisters, a Black Madonna, and a stunning array of reliquaries and monstrances.

P.58 ▸ HRADČANY

▼ Strahov Monastery

Strahov boasts two monastic libraries with fantastically ornate bookshelves and colourful frescoes.

P.59 ▸ HRADČANY

Restaurants

Czech cuisine is not the world's most revered, and the stuff that was produced by the country's chefs under the Communists didn't further the cause. However, Prague's restaurants have come a long way in the last two decades. You can now sample cuisines from around the world, from Afghan to Vietnamese, though it's still easier to find elegant surroundings than to eat truly memorable food.

▲ **Mlýnec**

Top-class food and a superb view over the Charles Bridge and the Castle.

P.85 ▶ STARÉ MĚSTO

◀ Pravda

Fashionable clientele, excellent service and an eclectic oriental menu.

P.94 ▸ STARÉ MĚSTO

▼ Kampa Park

Fish and seafood restaurant exquisitely located by the river.

P.70 ▸ MALÁ STRANA

◀ Zahrada v opeře

Global cuisine beautifully presented at reasonable prices and served in the former stock exchange.

P.102 ▸ WENCESLAS SQUARE AND NORTHERN NOVÉ MĚSTO

▼ Kogo

Popular pasta and pizza place in Staré Město.

P.85 ▸ STARÉ MĚSTO

Cafés

At the beginning of the twentieth century, Prague boasted a café society to rival that of Vienna or Paris. A handful of these classic, ornate Habsburg-era haunts have survived, or been resurrected, and should definitely be sampled. In addition, Prague has a small number of teahouses (*ajovny*), a peculiarly Czech institution, with an equally long pedigree. These places range from smoke-free, Zen-style havens to chill-out zones complete with hookahs. The tea-drinking is taken very seriously and there's usually a staggering array of leaves on offer.

▼ Obecní dům

Café decor doesn't come better than this Art Nouveau masterpiece.

P.101 ▶ WENCESLAS SQUARE AND NORTHERN NOVÉ MĚSTO

▲ Grand Café Orient

Perfect reconstruction of a first-floor Cubist café from 1911.

P.84 ▶ WENCESLAS SQUARE AND NORTHERN NOVÉ MĚSTO

▲ Montmartre

Vaulted former haunt of the likes of Kafka, Werfel and Hašek.

P.84 ▶ STARÉ MĚSTO

▼ Dahab

The most spacious and extravagant of the city's teahouses also serves tasty Middle Eastern snacks.

P.84 ▶ STARÉ MĚSTO

▼ Café Louvre

First-floor café that roughly reproduces its illustrious 1902 predecessor.

P.109 ▶ NÁRODNÍ AND SOUTHERN NOVÉ MĚSTO

Museums and galleries

With so much glorious art and architecture on the streets of Prague, many visitors happily skip the city's museums and galleries in favour of the city itself. But it would be a shame not to sample what Prague's museums and galleries have to offer, from medieval art and internationally renowned Czech painters Krupka and Mucha, to the Czech Cubist movement and the Veletržní Palace, with its comprehensive overview of Czech and European art of the last two centuries.

▲ Mucha Museum

Dedicated to Alfons Mucha, the Czech artist best known for his Parisian posters.

P.98 › WENCESLAS SQUARE AND NORTHERN NOVÉ MĚSTO

▲ Veletržní Palace

The city's premier modern art museum is housed in the functionalist Trade Fair Palace.

P.121 › HOLEŠOVICE

▼ UPM

A treasure-trove of Czech applied art ranging from Meissen porcelain and Art Nouveau vases to avant-garde photography.

P.92 ▶ JOSEFOV

▼ Museum of Cubism

Czech artists, sculptors and architects were at the forefront of the Cubist movement.

P.81 ▶ STARÉ MĚSTO

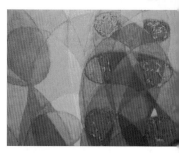

▲ Museum Kampa

Private collection housed in a converted watermill and stuffed with works by František Kupka, among others.

P.66 ▶ MALÁ STRANA

▲ Convent of St Agnes

Gothic convent that provides the perfect setting for the national collection of medieval art.

P.80 ▶ STARÉ MĚSTO

Churches

The two golden ages of church building in Prague were the late medieval and Baroque periods. The city's Gothic cathedral was begun in the reign of Charles IV in the fourteenth century, as was the Týn church, but like many of Prague's churches, both now have plenty of Baroque furnishings. To sample the high point of Prague Baroque, head for the Church of sv Mikuláš, built from scratch in the eighteenth century.

▼ Panna Maria Vítězná

Home of the *Bambino di Praga*, the pint-sized wax effigy of Jesus that boasts a vast wardrobe.

P.67 ▸ MALÁ STRANA

▼ Church of sv Ignác

Ornate Jesuit church modelled on Il Gesù, their headquarters in Rome.

P.107 ▸ NÁRODNÍ AND SOUTHERN NOVÉ MĚSTO

▲ Church of sv Mikuláš

The city's finest Baroque church, whose dome and tower dominate the skyline of Malá Strana.

P.62 ▸ MALÁ STRANA

▼ Church of sv Jakub

Colourful frescoes plastered over Gothic vaulting, and the mother of all church organs.

P.79 ▸ STARÉ MĚSTO

▼ Cathedral of sv Vít

Prague's cathedral stands in the middle of the castle and took centuries to complete.

P.49 ▸ PRAGUE CASTLE

▲ Týn church

Fairy-tale Gothic church whose twin towers rise up above the gables of Old Town Square.

P.79 ▸ STARÉ MĚSTO

Literary Prague

From Kafka and Rilke and the Good Soldier Švejk to Havel, the playwright-turned-president, Prague has a rich and unusual literary pedigree. The tourist industry may have flogged Kafka to death, and ruined Jaroslav Hašek's local, but there are still plenty of literary associations that have yet to be fully exploited.

▲ Old-New Synagogue

The Golem, a sort of Jewish Frankenstein, reputedly still lives above the Old-New Synagogue.

P.88 ▸ JOSEFOV

▼ U zlatého tygra

Bohemian writer Bohumil Hrabal's local is still frequented by his old friends.

P.86 ▸ STARÉ MĚSTO

▲ Café Slavia

Immortalized in a poem by Nobel Prize-winner Jaroslav Seifert, this café is haunted by the ghosts of generations of Czech writers.

P.110 ▸ NÁRODNÍ AND SOUTHERN NOVÉ MĚSTO

▼ Old Royal Palace (Vladislav Hall)

It was here that absurdist playwright Václav Havel was sworn in as president.

P.52 ▸ PRAGUE CASTLE

▲ Franz Kafka

Few cities are as closely associated with one writer as Prague is with Franz Kafka, who was born and spent most of his life in the city.

P.88 ▸ JOSEFOV

Kids' Prague

Despite the lack of hands-on interactive attractions, most kids will love Prague, with its hilly cobbled streets and trams, especially in the summer when the place is positively alive with street performers and buskers. Prague Castle rarely disappoints either, with colourfully clad guards and lots of fairy-tale ramparts and towers. The other obvious attractions for children are the Petřín hill, with its funicular and mirror maze; the zoo; and the National Technical Museum with its trains, planes and automobiles.

▼ Prague Zoo

Prague Zoo occupies an attractive hilly site north of Prague and is a guaranteed winner with all youngsters.

P.126 ▸ HOLEŠOVICE

▲ Petřín

This wooded hill gives kids a chance to run around, has fabulous views and an anti-quated mirror maze.

P.68 ▶ MALÁ STRANA

◀ Museum of Miniatures

Marvel at the smallest book in the world or the Lord's Prayer written on a human hair.

P.59 ▶ HRADČANY

▶ Ice cream at Cremeria Milano

Cheap Czech *zmrzlina* outlets stand aside, a real Italian *gelateria* has opened in Prague.

P.93 ▶ JOSEFOV

▼ Changing of the Guard

With a lilting modern fanfare and toytown soldiers, Prague's Changing of the Guard is funky like no other.

P.49 ▶ PRAGUE CASTLE

Classical Prague

The Czechs have produced four top-drawer composers – Dvořák, Smetana, Janáček and Martinů – and although none hails from Prague, the legacy of their music still dominates the cultural scene here. Dvořák and Smetana both have museums dedicated to them and are buried in the illustrious Vyšehrad Cemetery. Prague is also rich in Mozart associations – after the success of *Figaro* here, the young composer went on to premiere two of his operas in the city's main opera house.

▲ Rudolfinum

One-time seat of the Czechoslovak Parliament, now home to the Czech Philharmonic.

P.92 ▸ JOSEFOV

▲ Prague State Opera

The 1888 former New German Theatre is now Prague's number two opera house.

P.102 ▸ WENCESLAS SQUARE AND NORTHERN NOVÉ MĚSTO

▼ Obecní dům

This Art Nouveau concert hall is the main venue for the Prague Spring Festival.

P.102 ▸ WENCESLAS SQUARE AND NORTHERN NOVÉ MĚSTO

▼ Estates Theatre

The city's chief opera house has a glittering interior and many Mozart associations.

P.86 ▸ STARÉ MĚSTO

▲ Dvořák Museum

The most famous Czech composer of all time is commemorated in this delightful Baroque villa.

P.116 ▸ NÁRODNÍ AND SOUTHERN NOVÉ MĚSTO

▲ Vyšehrad Cemetery

Resting place of just about every Czech writer, artist and musician of renown.

P.115 ▸ VYŠEHRAD, VINOHRADY AND ŽIŽKOV

Art Nouveau Prague

The emergence of Art Nouveau in Paris, with its curvaceous sculptural decoration and floral motifs, had an enormous impact on Prague's architects in the 1890s. Later, a more restrained, rectilinear style that prefigured early modernism, arrived via the Secession movement (*secesní*) in Vienna. And thanks to the lack of war damage and postwar redevelopment, virtually all of Prague's Art Nouveau treasures have remained intact.

▼ Mucha window

The modern furnishings in Prague's cathedral include two stained-glass windows by Alfons Mucha.

P.49 ▸ PRAGUE CASTLE

▼ Obecní dům

Built in 1911 with the help of the leading Czech artists of the day, this is the city's finest Art Nouveau edifice.

P.98 ▸ WENCESLAS SQUARE AND NORTHERN NOVÉ MĚSTO

▲ Grand Hotel Evropa

A bit worn at the edges, the Evropa's café nevertheless retains its original 1905 decor.

P.101 ▸ WENCESLAS SQUARE AND NORTHERN NOVÉ MĚSTO

▼ Jan Hus Monument

This gargantuan Art Nouveau monument forms the centrepiece of Old Town Square.

P.78 ▸ STARÉ MĚSTO

▼ Praha hlavní nádraží

Fight your way through the subterranean modern station and you'll find Josef Fanta's glorious 1909 station more or less intact.

P.99 ▸ WENCESLAS SQUARE AND NORTHERN NOVÉ MĚSTO

Pubs

When it comes to beer consumption, Czechs top the world league table. This comes as little surprise, since the pub (*pivnice* or *hostinec*) is the country's primary social institution and beers like Budvar and Pilsner Urquell are considered among the finest in the world. The traditional *pivnice* is a simple place, with long tables and benches and waiters who bring a constant supply of mugs of frothing beer. Such places are becoming harder to find in Prague, but enough remain for a decent pub crawl.

▼ U vystřelenýho oka

Archetypal smoky, hard-drinking Žižkov pub with unpronounceable name.

P.120 ▶ VYŠEHRAD, VINOHRADY AND ŽIŽKOV

▼ U kocoura

Old-established Malá Strana pub serving Budvar.

P.71 ▶ MALÁ STRANA

▲ Letenský zámeček

Great summer terrace overlooking the city and river from Letná.

P.128 ▸ HOLEŠOVICE

▶ U medvídků

One of the few central pubs to have changed little over the decades.

P.86 ▸ STARÉ MĚSTO

◀ U černého vola

A truly authentic unpretentious pub serving Velkopopovický kozel beer.

P.60 ▸ HRADČANY

▼ Pivovarský dům

Best of the city's new microbreweries with a good range of traditional pub food.

P.111 ▸ NÁRODNÍ AND SOUTHERN NOVÉ MĚSTO

Shops and markets

Despite the presence of the familiar multinational franchises, Prague still abounds in small, one-off independent shops, even in the centre. The city's secondhand, antique, bric-a-brac or junk shops are always worth a browse: the terms to look out for are *starožitnosti*, *antikvariát*, *bazar* and, believe it or not, "secondhand". The country is famous for its crystal and glassware, as well as garnet and amber jewellery. Other popular souvenir choices include traditional wooden toys and marionettes.

▲ Manufaktura

Chain store specializing in wooden and ceramic folk art, with branches all across the city centre.

P.83 ▸ STARÉ MĚSTO

▲ Botanicus

Prague's own home-grown version of the Body Shop.

P.82 ▸ STARÉ MĚSTO

▲ Cellarius

One of the best selections of Czech wines in the capital.

P.100 ▸ WENCESLAS SQUARE AND NORTHERN NOVÉ MĚSTO

▼ Kubista

Beautifully designed reproduction Czech Cubist pieces, primarily furniture and ceramics.

P.83 ▸ STARÉ MĚSTO

◄ Christmas markets

Cute arts and crafts stalls occupy the city's main squares in the run-up to Christmas each year.

P.146 ▸ STARÉ MĚSTO

Communist Prague

Despite forty-odd years of Communism, the regime left very few physical traces on the city. Understandably, the Czechs themselves aren't keen on harking back to those times, either. Yet if you know where to look, there are several understated – and one or two ironic – memorials to the period. For example, the giant metronome on Letná stands on the spot where the world's largest statue of Stalin once stood. And if you're still not sated, there's even a Museum of Communism, full of memorabilia.

▼ Museum of Communism

An enterprising museum that gives a glimpse into the country's Communist past.

P.97 ▶ WENCESLAS SQUARE AND NORTHERN NOVÉ MĚSTO

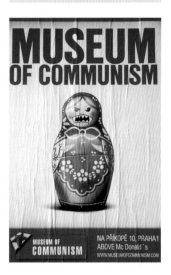

▼ Národní třída

It was the confrontation between police and protesters on this street that sparked the 1989 Velvet Revolution.

P.104 ▶ NÁRODNÍ AND SOUTHERN NOVÉ MĚSTO

▲ Míčovna

The Communist restorers of this Renaissance ball-games court left a discreet ideological stamp on their work.

P.55 ▸ PRAGUE CASTLE

▼ Kinský Palace

The 1948 Communist coup was declared on the palace balcony overlooking Old Town Square.

P.78 ▸ STARÉ MĚSTO

▼ Jan Palach memorial

In 1969 on Wenceslas Square, Jan Palach set fire to himself in protest against the Soviet invasion.

P.95 ▸ WENCESLAS SQUARE AND NORTHERN NOVÉ MĚSTO

▲ Memorial to the Victims of Communism

A visually striking, very modern memorial to those who suffered under the regime.

P.68 ▸ MALÁ STRANA

40

Views from on high

With its hilltop castle, its skyline of dreaming spires and domes, its winding river and centuries of architecture untouched by disasters natural or unnatural, Prague is central Europe's most photogenic city. Climb up to the castle or walk across the Charles Bridge, and you'll be blessed with wonderful views. For the ultimate rooftop or hilltop vantage points, however, you need to head for one of these strategic locations.

▲ Letná
The best place for a view of the River Vltava and its many bridges.

P.123 ▸ HOLEŠOVICE

▲ Žižkov Tower
Prague's futuristic TV tower is the city's tallest structure and the ultimate viewpoint.

P.117 ▸ VYŠEHRAD, VINOHRADY AND ŽIŽKOV

▼ Astronomical Tower, Klementinum

An unusual view over the rooftops of Staré Město.

P.73 ▸ STARÉ MĚSTO

▲ Staré Město Town Hall

Bird's-eye view of Prague's showpiece square and the crowds watching the astronomical clock.

P.77 ▸ STARÉ MĚSTO

▼ Cathedral of sv Vít

The cathedral's south tower gives you a great view over the castle and beyond to the rest of Prague.

P.49 ▸ PRAGUE CASTLE

▲ Petřín

The best view from Petřín hill is from Prague's own miniature version of the Eiffel Tower.

P.68 ▸ MALÁ STRANA

Nightlife

Many of Prague's pubs, bars and music venues stay open very late, so after midnight you're not necessarily committed to a full-on club. If you do go clubbing, you'll find a fairly modest choice of places, split between techno and top twenty. If you're lucky, you'll be able to simply walk home; otherwise, you'll find night trams run every thirty to forty minutes in every direction from Lazarská.

▲ Radost FX

Long-established basement club, with a veggie café upstairs.

P.120 ▸ VYŠEHRAD, VINOHRADY AND ŽIŽKOV

▲ Mecca

This coolly converted factory is one of the most impressive, professional and popular clubs in Prague.

P.128 ▸ HOLEŠOVICE

◀ Roxy

City-centre dance club with its finger in all sorts of avant-garde pies.

P.87 ▸ STARÉ MĚSTO

▶ Divadlo Archa

The most adventurous theatre in Prague, with everything from straight theatre to dance and live music.

P.102 ▸ WENCESLAS SQUARE AND NORTHERN NOVÉ MĚSTO

▼ AghaRTA Jazz Centrum

Prague's best venue for jazz and blues is situated just off Old Town Square.

P.86 ▸ NÁRODNÍ AND SOUTHERN NOVÉ MĚSTO

Twentieth-century architecture

Prague is renowned for its beautifully preserved Gothic, Baroque and Art Nouveau buildings. However, the city's twentieth-century architecture is less well known, but equally remarkable. The Czechs were the only ones to apply Cubism to buildings and later created a putative nationalist style – Rondo-Cubism. Their embrace of Functionalism in the interwar years drew praise from Le Corbusier himself, and today this legacy remains an important influence on the city's contemporary architecture.

▼ Cubist streetlamp

Delightfully whimsical lamppost and seat hidden away in Jungmannovo náměstí.

P.103 ▸ HRADČANY

▼ Plečník's church

A postmodern masterpiece by Slovene architect, Josip Plečník.

P.117 ▸ VYŠEHRAD, VINOHRADY AND ŽIŽKOV

▲ Baťa store

All prewar Baťa stores were designed along functionalist lines.

P.95 ▶ WENCESLAS SQUARE AND NORTHERN NOVÉ MĚSTO

▼ Banka legií

The city's finest Rondo-Cubist building contains a great frieze featuring the Czecho-slovak Legion.

P.99 ▶ WENCESLAS SQUARE AND NORTHERN NOVÉ MĚSTO

▲ Dancing House

Prague's most distinctive building from the 1990s.

P.108 ▶ NÁRODNÍ AND SOUTHERN NOVÉ MĚSTO

▼ Cubist villas

The most successful application of architectural Cubism in Prague.

P.116 ▶ VYŠEHRAD, VINOHRADY & ŽIŽKOV

Places

Prague Castle

Prague's skyline is dominated by the vast hilltop complex of Prague Castle (Pražský hrad), which looks out over the city centre from the west bank of the River Vltava. There's been a royal seat here for over a millennium, and it continues to serve as headquarters of the Czech president, but the castle is also home to several of Prague's chief tourist attractions: the Gothic Cathedral of sv Vít, the late medieval Old Royal Palace, the diminutive and picturesque Golden Lane, and numerous museums and galleries. The best thing about the place, though, is that the public are free to roam around the atmospheric courtyards and take in the views from ramparts from early in the morning until late at night.

Cathedral of sv Vít

Daily: April–Oct 9am–5pm; Nov–March 9am–4pm. Free. Begun by Emperor Charles IV (1346–78), the cathedral has a long and chequered history and wasn't finally completed until 1929. Once inside, it's difficult not to be impressed by the sheer height of the nave, and struck by the modern fixtures and fittings, especially the stained-

Visiting the castle

You're free to wander round the precincts of the castle (daily: April–Oct 5am–midnight; Nov–March 6am–11pm; ☎224 373 368, ⓦwww.hrad.cz). There are two main types of **multi-entry ticket** available for the sights within the castle (excluding the cathedral). The **long tour** ticket (350Kč) gives you entry to most of the sights within the castle: the Old Royal Palace, the Basilica and Convent of sv Jiří, the Prague Castle Picture Gallery and the Golden Lane. The **short tour** (250Kč) only covers the Old Royal Palace, the Basilica of sv Jiří, and the Golden Lane. Castle tickets are valid for two days and are available from various ticket offices including the main information centre in the third courtyard, opposite the cathedral. The Toy Museum and any temporary exhibitions such as those held in the Imperial Stables and Riding School all have separate admission charges.

Most people **approach the castle** from Malostranská metro station by taking the steep shortcut up the Staré zámecké schody, which brings you into the castle from the rear entrance to the east. A better approach is up the more stately Zámecké schody, where you can stop and admire the view before entering the castle via the main gates. From April to October, you might also consider coming up through Malá Strana's wonderful terraced gardens (see p.65), which are connected to the castle gardens. The alternative to all this climbing is to take tram #22 from Malostranská metro, which tackles a couple of hairpin bends before it deposits you at the Pražský hrad stop outside the Royal Gardens to the north of the castle.

The hourly **Changing of the Guard** at the main gates is a fairly subdued affair, but every day at noon there's a much more elaborate parade, accompanied by a modern fanfare.

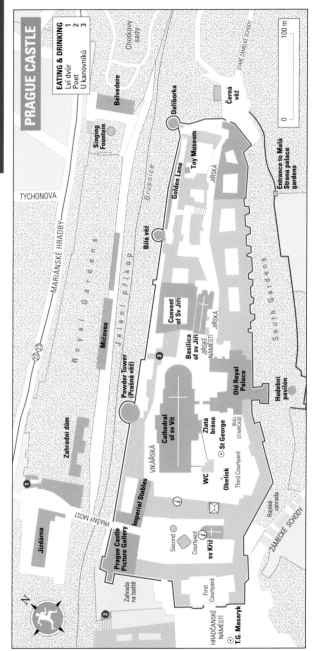

PRAGUE CASTLE

EATING & DRINKING	
Lví dvůr	1
Poet	2
U kanovníků	3

0 ━━━━━━━━ 100 m

Chotkovy sady

Belvedere

STARÉ ZÁMECKÉ SCHODY

Singing Fountain

Dalibořka

Černá věž

Toy Museum

Golden Lane

Entrance to Malá Strana palace gardens

JIŘSKÁ

TYCHONOVA

Brusnice

Bílá věž

MARIÁNSKÉ HRADBY

Royal Gardens

Míčovna

Jelení příkop

Convent of Sv Jiří

South Gardens

Zahradní dům

Powder Tower (Prašná věž)

3

Basilica of sv Jiří

JIŘSKÉ NÁMĚSTÍ

JIŘSKÁ

12·22

VIKÁŘSKÁ

Cathedral of sv Vít

Zlatá brána

Old Royal Palace

Hudební pavilón

Imperial Stables

WC

St George

BULL STAIRCASE

Jízdárna

Obelisk

Third Courtyard

PRAŠNÝ MOST

1

Second Courtyard

2

sv Kříž

Rajská zahrada

ZÁMECKÉ SCHODY

Prague Castle Picture Gallery

Zahrada na baště

First Courtyard

2

HRADČANSKÉ NÁMĚSTÍ

T.G. Masaryk

▲ BATTLING TITANS

unfolds above the cornice in sixteenth-century paintings.

The highlight of the chancel is the **Tomb of St John of Nepomuk**, a work of Baroque excess, sculpted in solid silver with free-flying angels holding up the heavy drapery of the baldachin. On the lid of the tomb, back-to-back with John himself, a cherub points to the martyr's severed tongue. Before you leave the chancel, check out the Habsburgs' sixteenth-century marble **Imperial Mausoleum**, in the centre of the choir, surrounded by a fine Renaissance grille. Below lies the claustrophobic **Royal Crypt**, resting place of emperors Charles IV and Rudolf II, plus various other Czech kings and queens.

From noon, you can also climb the cathedral's **Great Tower** from the south aisle. Outside the cathedral, don't forget to clock the Golden Gate, above the south door, decorated with a remarkable fourteenth-century mosaic of the Last Judgement.

glass windows, among them Alfons Mucha's superb *Cyril and Methodius* window, in the third chapel in the north wall, and František Bílek's wooden altar, in the north aisle.

Of the cathedral's numerous side chapels, the grand **Chapel of sv Václav** (better known as Wenceslas, of "Good King" fame), by the south door, is easily the main attraction. The country's patron saint was killed by his pagan brother, Boleslav the Cruel, who later repented, converted, and apparently transferred his brother's remains to this very spot. The chapel's gilded walls are inlaid with over a thousand semiprecious stones, set around ethereal fourteenth-century frescoes of the Passion; meanwhile the tragedy of Wenceslas

Old Royal Palace (Starý královský palác)

Daily: April–Oct 9am–5pm; Nov–March 9am–4pm. 140Kč. The Old Royal Palace is a sandwich of royal apartments, built one on top of the other by successive princes and kings of Bohemia, but left

▲ CHANGING OF THE GUARD

largely unfurnished and unused for the last three hundred years. Immediately past the antechamber is the bare expanse of the **Vladislav Hall**, with its remarkable, sweeping rib-vaulting which forms floral patterns on the ceiling, the petals reaching almost to the floor. It was here that the early Bohemian kings were elected, and since 1918 every president has been sworn into office in the hall. From a staircase in the southwest corner, you can climb up to the Bohemian Chancellery, scene of Prague's **second defenestration**, when two Catholic governors appointed by Ferdinand I were thrown out of the window by a group of Protestant Bohemian noblemen in 1618. A quick canter down the Riders' Staircase will take you to the Gothic and Romanesque palace chambers containing "The Story of Prague Castle",

▲ CATHEDRAL DOOR

an interesting, if overlong, exhibition on the development of the castle through the centuries.

Basilica of sv Jiří

Jiřské náměstí. Daily: April–Oct 9am–5pm; Nov–March 9am–4pm. Don't be fooled by the basilica's russet-red Baroque facade, which dominates the square; inside is Prague's most beautiful Romanesque building, meticulously scrubbed clean and restored to re-create something like the honey-coloured stone basilica that replaced the original tenth-century church in 1173. The double staircase to the chancel is a remarkably harmonious late Baroque addition and now provides a perfect stage for chamber music concerts. The choir vault contains a rare early thirteenth-century painting of the New Jerusalem from Revelation, while to the right of the chancel are sixteenth-century frescoes of the burial chapel of sv Ludmila, Bohemia's first Christian martyr and grandmother of St Wenceslas.

Convent of sv Jiří (Jiřský klášter)

Jiřské náměstí ⓦ www.ngprague.cz. Daily 10am–6pm. 100Kč. Founded in 973, Bohemia's earliest monastery was closed down in 1782, and now houses an art gallery. The collection is of limited interest to the non-specialist, and is due to move to the Schwarzenberg Palace (see p.56) in 2008. The collection includes the overtly sensual and erotic Mannerist paintings that prevailed during the reign of Rudolf II (1576–1612), while the rest comprises a vast collection of Czech Baroque art, by the likes of Bohemia's Karel Škréta and Petr Brandl and the great sculptors Matthias Bernhard Braun and Ferdinand Maximilian Brokof.

▲ BULL STAIRCASE

Golden Lane
(Zlatá ulička)
Daily: April–Oct 9am–5pm; Nov–March 9am–4pm. A seemingly blind alley of brightly coloured miniature cottages, Golden Lane is by far the most popular sight in the castle, and during the day, at least, the whole street is crammed with sightseers. Originally built in the sixteenth century for the 24 members of Rudolf II's castle guard, the lane allegedly takes its name from the goldsmiths who followed a century later. By the nineteenth century, the whole street had become a kind of palace slum, attracting artists and craftsmen, its two most famous inhabitants being Nobel Prize-winning poet Jaroslav Seifert and Franz Kafka, who came here in the evenings to write short stories during the winter of 1916.

Toy Museum
(Muzeum hraček)
Jiřská 4. Daily 9.30am–5.30pm. 100Kč. With brief captions and unimaginative displays, this museum is a disappointing venture, which fails to live up to its potential. The collection is certainly impressive in its range, containing everything from toy cars and motorbikes to robots and even Barbie dolls, but there are only a few buttons for younger kids to press, and unless you're really lost for something to do, or have a specialist interest in toys, you could happily skip the whole enterprise.

Lobkowicz Palace
(Lobkovický palác)
Jiřská 3 ⊛www.lobkowiczevents.cz. Daily 10.30am–6pm. 275Kč. Appropriated in 1948 and only recently handed back, the Lobkowicz Palace now houses a pricey new exhibition (with audioguide accompaniment) on the Lobkowicz family, as well as displaying a fair selection of

PLACES Prague Castle

▲ ST GEORGE AND THE DRAGON

their prize possessions, including original manuscripts by Mozart and Beethoven, old musical instruments, arms and armour and one or two masterpieces by the likes of Velázquez, Canaletto and Brueghel the Elder.

Powder Tower (Prašná věž)

Vikářská. Daily: April–Oct 9am–5pm; Nov–March 9am–4pm. Also known as Mihulka after the lamprey (*mihule*), an eel-like fish supposedly bred here for royal consumption, the tower is actually more noteworthy as the place where Rudolf's team of alchemists were put to work trying to discover the secret of the philosopher's stone. Despite its colourful history, the exhibition currently on display within the tower is rather dull, with just a pair of furry slippers and a hat belonging to Emperor Ferdinand I to get excited about.

South Gardens (Jižní zahrady)

April–Oct daily 10am–6pm. Free. These gardens enjoy wonderful vistas over the city and link up with the terraced gardens of Malá Strana (see p.65).

Originally laid out in the sixteenth century, the gardens were thoroughly remodelled in the 1920s with the addition of an observation terrace and colonnaded pavilion, below which is an earlier eighteenth-century *Hudební pavilón* (music pavilion). Two sandstone obelisks further east record the arrival of the two Catholic councillors after their 1618 defenestration from the Royal Palace (see p.52).

Prague Castle Picture Gallery (Obrazárna pražského hradu)

Daily 10am–6pm. 140Kč. The remnants of the imperial collection, begun by Rudolf II, are housed here. Among the collection's finest paintings is Rubens' richly coloured *Assembly of the Gods at Olympus*, an illusionist triple portrait of Rudolf and his Habsburg predecessors that's typical of the sort of tricksy work that appealed to the emperor. Elsewhere, there's an early, very beautiful *Young Woman at Her Toilet* by Titian, and Tintoretto's *Flagellation of Christ*, a late work in which the artist makes very effective and dramatic use of light.

▲ SOUTH GARDENS

Imperial Stables (Císařská konírna)

Tues–Sun 10am–6pm. The former Imperial Stables lie on the opposite side of the courtyard to the picture gallery and still boast their original, magnificent Renaissance vaulting dating from the reign of Rudolf II. They are now used to house the castle's most prestigious temporary art exhibitions (admission fees vary).

Royal Gardens (Královská zahrada)

April–Oct daily 10am–6pm. Founded by Ferdinand I in 1530, the Royal Gardens are among the capital's most pristinely kept verdant green spaces, with fully functioning fountains and immaculately cropped lawns. It's a very popular spot, though more a place for admiring the azaleas and almond trees than lounging around on the grass. Set into the south terrace – from which there are unrivalled views over the cathedral – is the Renaissance ball-game court (Míčovna), occasionally open to the public for concerts and exhibitions. The walls are tattooed with sgraffito and feature a hammer and sickle to the side of one of the sandstone half-columns, thoughtfully added by restorers in the 1950s.

Belvedere

Tues–Sun 10am–6pm. Prague's most celebrated Renaissance building is a delicately arcaded summerhouse topped by an inverted copper ship's hull, begun by Ferdinand I in 1538 for his wife, Anne (though she didn't live long enough to see it completed). The Belvedere's exterior walls are decorated by a series of lovely figural reliefs depicting scenes from mythology, while the interior is used for exhibitions by contemporary artists. In the palace's miniature formal garden is the so-called Singing Fountain, named for the musical sound the drops of water make when falling in the metal bowls below.

Cafés

Poet

Na baště. Daily 11am–6pm. The best of the rather undistinguished castle cafés, tucked away by the northwestern ramparts, with tables on the outside terrace.

U kanovníků

Jiřské náměstí 35–36. Daily 11am–6pm. This café has good views overlooking the woody Stag Ditch, and is a good warm spot for a winter coffee stop – if you can get a table.

▲ FILIGREE IRONWORK AT PRAGUE CASTLE

Restaurants

Lví dvůr (Lion's Court)

U prašného mostu 6 ☎ 224 372 361, ⊛ www.lvidvur.cz. Daily 11am–midnight. Housed in what used to be Rudolf II's private zoo, with a terrace overlooking the Royal Gardens and the cathedral, this smart restaurant serves up roast hog and plenty of other Czech specialities, with main dishes from 250Kč.

Hradčany

The monumental scale and appearance of Hradčany – the district immediately outside Prague's castle – is a direct result of the great fire of 1541, which destroyed the small-scale medieval houses that once stood here and allowed the Habsburg nobility to transform Hradčany into the grand architectural showpiece it still is. Nowadays, despite the steady stream of tourists en route to the castle, it's also one of the most peaceful parts of central Prague, barely disturbed by the civil servants who work in the area's numerous ministries and embassies. The three top sights to head for are the Šternberg Palace, with its modest collection of Old Masters, the Baroque pilgrimage church of Loreto and the ornate libraries of the Strahov monastery.

Hradčanské náměstí

Hradčanské náměstí fans out from the castle gates, surrounded by the oversized palaces of the old Catholic nobility. The one spot everyone heads for is the ramparts in the southeastern corner, which allow an unrivalled view over the red rooftops of Malá Strana, and beyond. Few people make use of the square's central green patch, which is heralded by a wonderful giant green wrought-iron lamppost from the 1860s and, behind it, a Baroque plague column. The most noteworthy palaces on the square are the **Schwarzenberg Palace**, at no. 2, with its over-the-top sgraffito decoration; the sumptuous, vanilla-coloured Rococo **Archbishop's Palace**, opposite; and the Martinic Palace, at no. 8 in the far northwestern corner of the square, whose sgraffito exterior features, among other scenes, Potiphah's wife trying to tempt young Joseph.

Museum of Mechanical Musical Instruments

Hradčanské náměstí 12 ⓦ www. orchestriony.cz. Daily 9am–6pm. 100Kč. Hradčanské náměstí is also home to probably the most enjoyable museum in the castle area, comprising three rooms stuffed with an impressive collection of antique mechanical instruments, from café orchestrions and fairground barrel organs to early wax phonographs and portable gramophones. Best of all, though, is the fact that almost every exhibit is in working order – as the curators will demonstrate. The museum has a particularly fine array of music boxes, as well as several much rarer polyphones such as manopans, aristons and mignons, not to mention an original Edison Dictaphone from 1877.

Šternberg Palace

Hradčanské náměstí 15 ⓦ www. ngprague.cz. Tues–Sun 10am–6pm. 150Kč. This elegant early eighteenth-century palace is now used as an art gallery housing European Old Masters

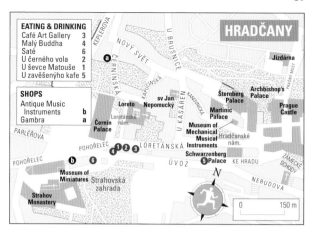

from the fourteenth to the eighteenth century. It's a modest collection in comparison with those of other major European capitals, though the handful of masterpieces makes a visit here worthwhile, and there's an elegant café in the courtyard.

The highlights of the first floor include Dieric Bouts' *Lamentation*, a complex composition crowded with figures in medieval garb, two richly coloured Bronzino portraits, and Jan Gossaert's eye-catching *St Luke Drawing the Virgin*, an exercise in architectural geometry and perspective. Before you head upstairs though, don't miss the side room (11) containing Orthodox icons from Venice, the Balkans and Russia.

The second floor boasts a searching portrait of old age by Tintoretto, a wonderfully rugged portrait by Goya and a mesmerizing *Praying Christ* by El Greco. Be sure to admire the Čínský kabinet, a small oval

chamber smothered in gaudy Baroque Chinoiserie, and one of the palace's few surviving slices of original decor. Elsewhere, there are a series of canvases by the Brueghel family, a Rembrandt and Rubens' colossal *Murder of St Thomas* (room 30).

The ground floor contains several superb Cranach canvases, plus one of the most celebrated paintings in the whole collection: the *Feast of the Rosary* by Albrecht Dürer, one of Rudolf II's most prized acquisitions, which he had transported on foot across the Alps to Prague.

▼ ČERNÍN PALACE

Černín Palace

Loretánské náměstí 5 www.
czechembassy.org. Loretánské
náměstí is dominated by the
phenomenal 135-metre-long
facade of the Černín Palace
(closed to the public), decorated
with thirty Palladian half-
columns and supported by a
swathe of diamond-pointed
rustication. Begun in the 1660s,
the building nearly bankrupted
future generations of Černíns,
who were eventually forced to
sell the palace to the Austrian
state in 1851, which converted it
into military barracks.

Since 1918, the palace has
housed the **Ministry of Foreign
Affairs**, and during World War
II it was, for a while, the Nazi
Reichsprotektor's residence.
On March 10, 1948, it was
the scene of Prague's third
– and most widely mourned
– defenestration. Only days
after the Communist coup, **Jan
Masaryk**, the only son of the
founder of Czechoslovakia,
and the last non-Communist
in the cabinet, plunged to
his death from the top-floor
bathroom window of the palace.
Whether it was suicide (he had
been suffering from bouts of
depression, partly
induced by
the country's
political path)
or murder will
probably never
be satisfactorily
resolved, but
for most people
Masaryk's
death cast a
dark shadow
over the newly
established
regime.

Loreto

Loretánské náměstí 7 www.
loreta.cz. Tues–Sun 9am–12.15pm
& 1–4.30pm. 110Kč. The outer
casing of the Loreto church
was built in the early part of
the eighteenth century – all hot
flourishes and Baroque twirls,
topped by a belltower that clanks
out the hymn "We Greet Thee
a Thousand Times" on its 27
Dutch bells. The focus of the
pilgrimage complex is the **Santa
Casa** (a mock-up of Mary's home
in Nazareth), built in 1626 and
smothered in a rich mantle of
stucco depicting the building's
miraculous transportation from
the Holy Land. Pride of place
within is given to a limewood
statue of the Black Madonna and
Child, encased in silver.

Behind the Santa Casa, the
much larger Church of the
Nativity has a high cherub count,
plenty of Baroque gilding and a
lovely organ replete with music-
making angels and putti. You
can get some idea of the Loreto's
serious financial backing in the
church's treasury, whose master
exhibit is a tasteless Viennese
silver monstrance, studded
with diamonds taken from the
wedding dress of Countess

▼ TELESCOPE OVERLOOKING ROOFTOPS FROM STRAHOW MONASTERY

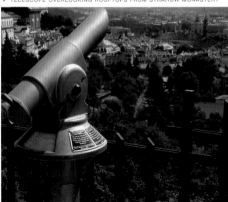

Kolovrat, who made the Loreto sole heir to her fortune.

Strahov Monastery

Strahovské nadvoří 1 ⓦwww. strahovmonastery.cz. Libraries: daily 9am–noon & 1–5pm. 80Kč. Gallery: Tues–Sun 9am–noon & 12.30–5pm. 60Kč. Founded in 1140 by the Premonstratensian order, the Baroque entrance to the Strahov Monastery is topped by a statue of its founder St Norbert, whose relics were brought here in 1627. The twelfth-century monastery church was remodelled in Baroque times and is well worth a peek for its colourful frescoes relating to St Norbert's life.

It's the monastery's two ornate Baroque **libraries**, though, that are the real reason for visiting Strahov. The Philosophical Hall has walnut bookcases so tall they almost touch the frescoes on the library's lofty ceiling, while the paintings on the low-ceilinged Theological Hall are framed by wedding-cake-style stuccowork.

The monastery's collection of religious art, church plate and reliquaries is displayed in the **Strahov Gallery** above the cloisters, and contains one or two gems: a portrait of Emperor Rudolf II by his court painter, Hans von Aachen, plus a superb portrait of Rembrandt's elderly mother by Gerrit Dou.

Museum of Miniatures

Strahovské nadvoří 11 ☎233 352 371, ⓦwww.muzeumminiatur. com. Daily 9am–5pm. 50Kč. The Strahov Monastery's most unusual attraction is set in the northeastern corner of the main courtyard. Displayed in this small museum are forty or so works by Anatoly Konyenko, a Russian who holds the record for constructing the smallest book in the world, a thirty-page edition of Chekhov's *Chameleon*. Among the other miracles of miniature manufacture are a (real, though dead) flea bearing golden horseshoes, scissors, and a key and lock; the Lord's Prayer written on a human hair; and a caravan of camels passing through the eye of a needle.

▲ HRADČANSKÉ NÁMĚSTÍ

Shops

Antique Music Instruments

Pohořelec 9. Daily 10am–6pm. More than just old violins, this place also sells icons, Art Nouveau glass, clocks and model trains – although at higher-than-average prices.

Gambra

Černínská 5. March–Oct Wed–Sun noon–6pm; Nov–Feb Sat & Sun noon–5.30pm. The commercial gallery of Prague's small but dogged Surrealist movement, past and present, also provides a window for the works of the late animator extraordinaire, Jan Švankmajer, and his wife, the artist Eva Švankmajerová, who live nearby.

▲ LORETO

Restaurants

Saté

Pohořelec 3 ☎ 220 514 552. Daily 11am–10pm. Simple, inexpensive veggie and non-veggie noodle and saté dishes with a vaguely Indonesian bent for around 100Kč.

U ševce Matouše (The Cobbler Matouš)

Loretánské náměstí 4 ☎ 220 514 536. Daily 11am–4pm & 6–11pm. Large steak and chips, for around 300Kč, is the speciality of this former cobbler's, which is one of the few half-decent places to eat in the castle district.

Cafés

Café Art Gallery

Loretánská náměstí 23. Daily 9am–7pm. Situated in the arcades south of Loretanské náměstí and serving excellent croissants, cakes, strudels, baguettes, sandwiches and very good coffee.

Malý Buddha

Úvoz 46. Tues–Sun 1–10.30pm. Typical Prague teahouse decor, with a Buddhist altar in one corner and good vegetarian Vietnamese snacks on the menu. A very useful smoke-free Hradčany haven.

U zavěšenýho kafe (The Hanging Café)

Úvoz 6. Daily 11am–midnight. A pleasant, smoky crossover café/pub serving cheap beer and traditional Czech food in a handy spot near the Hrad.

Pubs

U černého vola (The Black Ox)

Loretánské náměstí 1. Daily 10am–10pm. Great traditional Prague pub doing a brisk business providing the popular light beer Velkopopovický kozel in huge quantities to thirsty local workers, soaked up with a few classic pub snacks.

▲ POHOŘELEC

Malá Strana

Malá Strana, Prague's picturesque "Little Quarter", sits below the castle and is in many ways the city's most entrancing area. Its peaceful, often hilly, cobbled back-streets have changed very little since Mozart walked them during his frequent visits to Prague between 1787 and 1791. They conceal a whole host of quiet terraced gardens, as well as the wooded Petřín Hill, which together provide the perfect inner-city escape in the summer months. The Church of sv Mikuláš, by far the finest Baroque church in Prague, and the Museum Kampa, with its unrivalled collection of works by František Kupka, are the two major sights.

Malostranské náměstí

Malostranské náměstí, Malá Strana's main square, is dominated and divided in two by the Baroque church of sv Mikuláš (see p.62). Trams and cars wind their way across the cobbles below the church, regularly dodged by a procession of people – some heading up the hill to the castle, others pausing at one of the numerous bars and restaurants hidden in the square's arcades and Gothic vaults. On the square's north side at no. 18, distinguished by its two little turrets and rather shocking pistachio and vanilla colour scheme, is the dům Smiřických, where, in 1618, the Protestant posse met to decide how to get rid of Emperor Ferdinand's Catholic councillors: whether to attack them with daggers, or, as they eventually attempted, to kill them by chucking them out of the window (see p.52) of the Old Royal Palace. Sněmovní, the side street which runs alongside the palace's western facade, takes its name from the **Sněmovna**, the Neoclassical palace at no. 4, which served as the provincial Diet in the nineteenth century,

the National Assembly of the First Republic in 1918, the Czech National Council after federalization in 1968, and, since 1993, as home to the Chamber of Deputies, the (more important) lower house of the Czech parliament.

▲ MALOSTRANSKÉ NÁMĚSTÍ

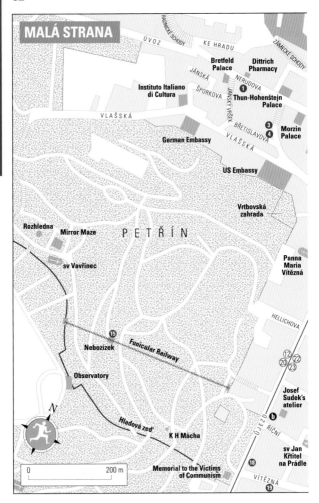

RADNICKÉ SCHODY
ÚVOZ
KE HRADU
ZÁMECKÉ SCHODY

Bretfeld Palace
Dittrich Pharmacy
JÁNSKÁ
NERUDOVA
Instituto Italiano di Cultura
ŠPORKOVA
Thun-Hohenštejn Palace
JÁNSKÝ VRŠEK
VLAŠSKÁ
BŘETISLAVOVA
Morzin Palace
German Embassy
VLAŠSKÁ

US Embassy

Vrtbovská zahrada

Rozhledna
Mirror Maze
P E T Ř Í N
Panna Maria Vítězná

sv Vavřinec
HELLICHOVA

Funicular Railway
Nebozízek
Josef Sudek's atelier

Observatory

ÚJEZD
ŘÍČNÍ

Hladová zeď
K H Mácha
sv Jan Křtitel na Prádle

Memorial to the Victims of Communism
VÍTĚZNÁ

N

0   200 m

Church of sv Mikuláš

Malostranské náměstí ⓦ www. psalterium.cz. Daily: March–Oct 9am–5pm; Nov–Feb 9am–4pm. 60Kč.

Towering over the whole of Malá Strana is the Baroque church of sv Mikuláš (St Nicholas), whose giant green dome and tower are among the most characteristic landmarks on Prague's left bank. Built by the Jesuits in the early eighteenth century, it was their most ambitious project yet in Bohemia, and the ultimate symbol of their stranglehold on the country. Nothing about the relatively plain west facade prepares you for the overwhelming High Baroque interior. The vast fresco in the nave portrays some of the more fanciful miraculous feats of St Nicholas, while the dome at the east end of the church is even

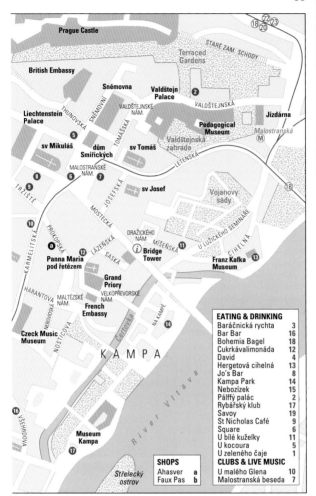

Prague Castle

STARÉ ZÁM. SCHODY

Terraced Gardens

British Embassy

Sněmovna

THUNOVSKÁ SNĚMOVNÍ

Valdštejn Palace

VALDŠTEJNSKÉ NÁM.

VALDŠTEJNSKÁ

Jízdárna

Liechtenstein Palace

TOMÁŠSKÁ

Pedagogical Museum

Malostranská (M)

sv Mikuláš

dům Smiřických

sv Tomáš

Valdštejnská zahrada

MALOSTRANSKÉ NÁM.

LETENSKÁ

TRŽIŠTĚ

JOSEFSKÁ

sv Josef

Vojanovy sady

PROKOPSKÁ

MOSTECKÁ

U LUŽICKÉHO SEMINÁŘE

DRAŽICKÉHO NÁM

ČIHELNA

KARMELITSKÁ

LÁZEŇSKÁ

SASKÁ

MÍŠEŇSKÁ

Bridge Tower

Panna Maria pod řetězem

Franz Kafka Museum

Grand Priory

HARANTOVA MALTÉZSKÉ NÁM.

VELKOPŘEVORSKÉ NÁM.

French Embassy

NEBOVIDSKÁ

ČERTOVKA

NA KAMPĚ

Czeck Music Museum

NOSTICOVA

KAMPA

River Vltava

VŠEHRDOVA

Museum Kampa

Střelecký ostrov

EATING & DRINKING

Baráčnická rychta	3
Bar Bar	16
Bohemia Bagel	18
Cukrkávalimonáda	12
David	4
Hergetová cihelná	13
Jo's Bar	8
Kampa Park	14
Nebozízek	15
Pálffý palác	2
Rybářský klub	17
Savoy	19
St Nicholas Café	9
Square	6
U bílé kuželky	11
U kocoura	5
U zeleného čaje	1
CLUBS & LIVE MUSIC	
U malého Glena	10
Malostranská beseda	7

SHOPS

Ahasver	a
Faux Pas	b

more impressive, thanks, more than anything, to its sheer height. Leering over you as you gaze up at the dome are four terrifyingly oversized and stern Church Fathers, one of whom brandishes a gilded thunderbolt, leaving no doubt as to the gravity of the Jesuit message. From April to October it's possible to climb the belfry for fine views over Malá Strana and the Charles Bridge.

Nerudova

The most important of the cobbled streets leading up to the castle is Nerudova. Historically, this was the city's main area for craftsmen, artisans and artists, though the shops and restaurants that line Nerudova now are mostly predictably and shamelessly aimed at tourists heading for the castle. Many of the houses that line the street

▲ U DVOU SLUNCŮ, NERUDOVA 47

retain their medieval barn doors and peculiar pictorial house signs. One of Nerudova's fancier buildings, at no. 5, is the Morzin Palace, now the Romanian Embassy, its doorway supported by two Moors (a pun on the owner's name). Meanwhile, two giant eagles hold up the portal of the Thun-Hohenštejn Palace, now the Italian Embassy. Further up the street, according to legend, Casanova and Mozart are said to have met up at a ball given by the aristocrat owners of no. 33, the Bretfeld Palace.

Dittrich Pharmacy

Nerudova 32. April–Sept Tues–Sun 11am–6pm; Oct–March Tues–Sun 10am–5pm. 20Kč. The old pharmacy, U zlatého lva (The Golden Lion), dating from 1821, has been restored to its former glory and now houses a small and mildly diverting exhibition whose prize exhibits are its leech bottles and a large dried-fruit fish.

Valdštejn Palace

Valdštejnské náměstí 4 ⓦ www.senat. cz. Built in the 1620s for Albrecht von Waldstein, commander of the Imperial Catholic armies of the Thirty Years' War, the Valdštejn Palace was one of the first and largest Baroque palaces in the city. Nowadays, it houses,

among other things, the Czech parliament's upper house, or **Senát**, which can be visited on a guided tour at weekends (Sat & Sun: April–Sept 10am–5pm; Oct–March 10am–4pm; free).

Pedagogical Museum

Valdštejn Palace ⓦ www.pmjak.cz. Tues–Sat 10am–12.30pm & 1–4.30pm 40Kč. The former palace stables contain the Pedagogical Museum, a small and old-fashioned exhibition on Czech education and, in particular, the influential teachings of Jan Amos Komenský (1592–1670) – better known as John Comenius – whose educational methods were revolutionary for their time.

Valdštejnská zahrada (Palace gardens)

April–Oct daily 10am–6pm. Free. The palace's formal gardens, the Valdštejnská zahrada – accessible from the palace's main entrance, and also from a doorway in the palace walls along Letenská – are a good place to take a breather from the city streets. The gardens' focus is a gigantic Italianate *sala terrena*, a monumental loggia decorated with frescoes of the Trojan Wars, which stands at the end of an avenue of sculptures. In addition, there are a number of peacocks, a pseudo grotto along the south wall, with quasi-stalactites, and a small aviary.

Valdštejnská jízdárna

Valdštejnská 1. Tues–Sun 10am–6pm. 100Kč. The palace's former riding school has been converted into a gallery, which puts on temporary exhibitions of fine art and photography organized by the National Gallery. It's accessible from the courtyard of nearby Malostranská metro station.

Terraced palace gardens

Valdštejnská. Daily: April & Oct 9am–6pm; May & Sept 9am–7pm; June & July 9am–9pm, Aug 9am–8pm. 80Kč. One of the chief joys of Malá Strana is its series of Baroque terraced gardens, on the slopes below the castle where the royal vineyards used to be. Dotted with urns and statuary, they command superb views over Prague. From Valdštejnská, you enter via the Ledeburská zahrada, gardens which eventually connect higher up with the castle's own South Gardens (see p.54).

Franz Kafka Museum

Cihelná 2b ⓦ www.kafkamuseum.cz. Daily 10am–6pm. 120Kč. This museum offers a fairly sophisticated rundown of Kafka's life and works. The first section includes photos of the old ghetto into which Kafka was born, an invoice from his father's shop, with the logo of a jackdaw (*kavka* in Czech), copies of his job applications, requests for sick leave, one of his reports on accident prevention in the workplace, and facsimiles of his pen sketches. Upstairs, audiovisuals and theatrical trickery are used to explore the torment, alienation and claustrophobia Kafka felt throughout his life and expressed in his writings.

Maltézské náměstí

Maltézské náměstí is one of a number of delightful little squares between Karmelitská and the river. At its centre is a plague column, topped by a statue of St John the Baptist, but the square takes its name from the Order of the Knights of St John of Jerusalem (better known by their later title, the Maltese

▲ TERRACED PALACE GARDENS

Knights), who in 1160 founded the nearby church of **Panna Maria pod řetězem** (St Mary below-the-chain), so called because it was the Knights' job to guard the Judith Bridge (predecessor to the Charles Bridge). Only two bulky Gothic towers are still standing and the apse is now thoroughly Baroque, but the nave remains unfinished and open to the elements.

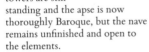

▲ Čertovka

John Lennon Wall

The Grand Priory of the Maltese Knights backs onto the pretty little square of Velkopřevorské náměstí, which echoes to the sound of music from the nearby Prague conservatoire. Following the violent death of John Lennon in 1980, Prague's youth established an ad hoc shrine smothered in graffiti tributes to the ex-Beatle along the Grand Priory's garden wall. The running battle between police and graffiti artists continued well into the 1990s, with the society of Maltese Knights taking an equally dim view of the mural, but a compromise has now been reached and the wall's scribblings legalized.

Kampa

Heading for Kampa, the largest of the Vltava's islands, with its cafés, old mills and serene riverside park, is the perfect way to escape the crowds. The island is separated from the left bank by Prague's "Little Venice", a thin strip of water called **Čertovka** (Devil's Stream), which used to power several mill-wheels until the last one ceased to function in 1936. For much of its history, the island was the city's main wash-house area, a fact commemorated by the church of sv Jan Křtitel na Prádle (St John-the-Baptist at the Cleaners) on Říční. It wasn't until the sixteenth and seventeenth centuries that the Nostitz family, who owned Kampa, began to develop the northern half of the island; the southern half was left untouched, and today is laid out as a public park, with riverside views across to Staré Město. To the north, the oval main square, Na Kampě, once a pottery market, is studded with slender acacia trees and cut through by the Charles Bridge, to which it is connected by a double flight of steps.

Museum Kampa

U Sovových mlýnů 2 ⓦ www. museumkampa.cz. Daily 10am–6pm. 120Kč, but free on Mon. Housed in an old riverside watermill, this museum is dedicated to the private art collection of Jan and Meda Mládek. As well as temporary exhibitions, the stylish modern gallery also houses the best of the Mládeks' collection, including a whole series of works by the Czech artist František

Kupka, seen by many as the father of abstract art. These range from early Expressionist watercolours to transitional pastels like *Fauvist Chair* from 1910, and more abstract works, such as the seminal oil painting, *Cathedral and Study for Fugue in Two Colours*, from around 1912. The gallery also displays a good selection of Cubist and later interwar works by the sculptor Otto Gutfreund and a few collages by postwar surrealist Jiří Kolář.

Vrtbovská zahrada

Karmelitská 25 ⓦ www.vrtbovska. cz. April–Oct daily 10am–6pm. 40Kč. One of the most elusive of Malá Strana's many Baroque gardens, the Vrtbovská zahrada was founded on the site of the former vineyards of the Vrtbov Palace. Laid out on Tuscan-style terraces, dotted with ornamental urns and statues of the gods by Matthias Bernhard Braun, the gardens twist their way up the lower slopes of Petřín Hill to an observation terrace from where there's a spectacular rooftop perspective on the city.

Church of Panna Maria Vítezná

Karmelitská 9 ⓦ www.pragjesu. com. Mon–Sat 9.40am–5.30pm, Sun 1–6pm. Free. Surprisingly, given its rather plain exterior, the church of Panna Maria Vítezná houses a high-kitsch wax effigy of the infant Jesus as a precocious three-year-old, enthroned in a glass case illuminated with strip-lights. Attributed with miraculous powers, this image, known as the **Bambino di Praga** (or Prazské Jezulátko), became an object of international pilgrimage and continues to attract visitors, as the multilingual prayer cards attest. The *bambino* boasts a vast

personal wardrobe of expensive swaddling clothes – approaching a hundred separate outfits at the last count – regularly changed by the Carmelite nuns. If you're keen to see some of these outfits, there's a small museum, up the spiral staircase in the south aisle, which contains his lacy camisoles, as well as a selection of his velvet and satin overgarments sent from all over the world.

Czech Music Museum

Karmelitská 2 ⓦ www.nm.cz. Daily except Tues 10am–6pm. 100Kč. Housed in a former nunnery, this museum's permanent collection begins with a crazy cut-and-splice medley of musical film footage from the last century. Next up is August Förster's pioneering quarter-tone grand piano from 1924 – you can even listen to Alois Hába's microtonal *Fantazie no. 10* composed for, and performed on, its three keyboards. After this rather promising start, the museum settles down into a conventional display of old central European instruments, from a precious Baumgartner clavichord and an Amati violin to Neapolitan mandolins and a vast contrabass over 2m in height. Best of all is the fact that you can hear many of the instruments on display being put through their paces at listening posts in each room.

Josef Sudek's Atelier

Újezd 30 ⓦ www.sudek-atelier.cz. Tues–Sun 10am–6pm. Free. Hidden behind the buildings on the east side of the Újezd is a faithful reconstruction of the cute little wooden garden studio, where Josef Sudek (1896–1976), the great Czech photographer, lived with his sister from 1927. Sudek moved out in 1958, but he used the place as his darkroom to the end of his life. The twisted tree in the front garden will be familiar to those acquainted with the numerous photographic cycles he based around the studio. The building has a few of Sudek's personal effects and is now used for temporary exhibitions of other photographers' works.

Memorial to the Victims of Communism

Corner of Újezd and Vítězná. In 2002, the Czechs finally erected a Memorial to the victims of Communism. The location has no particular resonance with the period, but the memorial itself has an eerie quality, especially when illuminated at night. It consists of a series of statues, self-portraits by sculptor Olbram Zoubek, standing on steps leading down from Petřín hill behind, each in varying stages of disintegration. The inscription at the base of the monument reads "205,486 convicted, 248 executed, 4500 died in prison, 327 annihilated at the border, 170,938 emigrated".

Petřín

The hilly wooded slopes of Petřín, distinguished by the Rozhledna, a scaled-down version of the Eiffel Tower, make up the largest green space in the city centre. The tower is just one of several exhibits which survive from the 1891 Prague Exhibition, whose modest legacy also includes the hill's funicular railway (see below). At the top of the hill, it's possible to trace the southernmost perimeter wall of the old city, popularly known as the **Hunger Wall** (Hladová zed). Instigated in the 1460s by Emperor Charles IV, it was much lauded at the time as a great public work which provided employment for the burgeoning

▲ FUNICULAR RAILWAY

ranks of the city's destitute (hence its name); in fact, much of the wall's construction was paid for by the expropriation of Jewish property.

Funicular railway

The funicular railway (*lanová dráha*) for Petřín sets off from a station just off Újezd and runs every 10–15min (daily 9.15am–8.45pm); public transport tickets and travel passes are valid. The Nebozízek stop halfway up gives access to *Nebozízek* restaurant pub (see p.70); the top station is closest to the Mirror Maze and Rozhledna.

Štefánik Observatory

Petřín 205 ⓦ www.observatory.cz. Tues–Sun, times vary. 40Kč. The Hunger Wall runs southeast from the funicular to Petřín's Štefánik Observatory. The small astronomical exhibition inside is hardly worth bothering with, but if it's a clear night, a quick peek through either of the observatory's two powerful telescopes is a treat.

Rozhledna

April daily 10am–5pm; May–Sept daily 10am–10pm; Oct daily 10am–6pm; Nov–March Sat & Sun 10am–5pm. 60Kč. Petřín's most familiar landmark is its look-out tower, or Rozhledna, an octagonal interpretation – though a mere fifth of the size – of the Eiffel Tower which shocked Paris in 1889, and a tribute to the city's strong cultural and political links with Paris at the time. The view from the public gallery is terrific in fine weather.

Mirror Maze (Bludiště)

April daily 10am–5pm; May–Sept daily 10am–10pm; Oct daily 10am–6pm; Nov–March Sat & Sun 10am–5pm. 50Kč. The Mirror Maze is housed in a mini neo-Gothic castle complete with mock drawbridge. As well as a mirror maze, there is an action-packed, life-sized diorama of the victory of Prague's students and Jews over the Swedes on the Charles Bridge in 1648. The humour of the convex and concave mirrors that lie beyond the diorama is so simple it has both adults and kids giggling away.

Shops

Ahasver

Prokopská 3 ⓦ www.ahasver.com. Tues–Sun 11am–6pm. Delightful little shop selling antique gowns and jewellery, as well as paintings, porcelain and glass.

Faux Pas

Újezd 26 ⓦ www.fauzpas.cz. Mon–Sat 11am–7pm. Designer Jolana Izbická goes in for brightly coloured and provocative clothing, as well as stocking one-off pieces by other central European designers.

▼ GERMAN EMBASSY, VLAŠSKÁ

Cafés

Bohemia Bagel

Újezd 16 ⓦ www.bohemiabagel.cz. Daily 7am–2am. Self-service expat favourite at the south end of Újezd, serving filled bagels, all-day breakfasts, soup and chilli. Internet access also available.

Cukrkávalimonáda

Lázeňská 7. Daily 8.30am–8pm. Very professional and well-run café, serving good brasserie-style dishes, as well as coffee and croissants, with tables overlooking the church of Panna Maria pod řetězem.

Savoy

Vítězná 5. Mon–Fri 8am–10.30pm, Sat & Sun 9am–10.30pm. This beautiful Habsburg-era café is also a very good place for seafood, thanks to the fishmonger's next door.

U zeleného caje (The Green Tea)

Nerudova 19. Daily 11am–10pm. Great little smoke-free stop-off for a pot of tea or a veggie snack en route to or from Prague Castle; the only problem is getting a place at one of the four tables.

Restaurants

Bar Bar

Všehrdova 17 ☎ 257 312 246. Mon–Thurs & Sun noon–midnight, Fri & Sat noon–2am. Unpretentious cellar restaurant with big, cheap salads (85–135Kč), savoury (mostly veggie) pancake dishes (around 100Kč) and sweet crêpes/palačinky on offer.

David

Tržiště 21 ☎ 257 533 109, ⓦ www. restaurant-david.cz. Tip-top service is guaranteed at this small, formal, family-run restaurant, which specializes in doing classic Bohemian cuisine full justice. Three-course fixed menus start at 500Kč.

Hergetová Cihelná

Cihelná 2b ☎ 296 826 103, ⓦ www. kampagroup.com. Daily 11.30am–1am. Slick, smart restaurant specializing in tiger prawn dishes (500Kč), plus tasty pizzas, pasta and risotto (250–350Kč). The riverside summer terrace overlooks Charles Bridge.

Kampa Park

Na Kampě 8b ☎ 296 826 102, ⓦ www. kampapark.com. Daily 11.30am–1am. Pink house exquisitely located right by the Vltava on Kampa Island, with a superb fish and seafood menu (mains 600–900Kč), top-class service and tables outside in summer.

Nebozízek (Little Auger)

Petřínské sady 411 ☎ 257 515 329, ⓦ www.nebozizek.cz. Daily 11am–11pm. Situated at the halfway stop on the Petřín funicular. The view is superb, there's an outdoor terrace and a traditional Czech menu heavy with game dishes for 300–400Kč.

Pálffý palác

Valdštejnská 14 ☎ 257 530 522, ⓦ www.palffy.cz. Daily 11am–11pm. Grand candle-lit room on the first floor of this old Baroque palace, and a wonderful outdoor terrace from which you can survey the red rooftops of Malá Strana. The international menu is renowned for its quail (main courses 500–700Kč).

Rybářský klub

U sovových mlýnů 1 ☎ 257 534 200. Daily noon–11pm. Freshwater fish – carp, catfish, zander and others – deep fried in breadcrumbs for around 300Kč are served up at this unpretentious riverside restaurant situated in the park on Kampa Island.

Square

Malostranské náměstí 5 ☎ 296 826 114, ⓦ www.kampagrooup.com. Daily 8am–1am. This once famous turn-of-the-century café has changed beyond all recognition – it's now a very smart bar and restaurant, serving an imaginative and well-executed, mostly Italian, menu, with pasta dishes, salads and main courses for 300–500Kč.

Pubs and bars

Baráčnická rychta
Na tržiště 23. Daily noon–midnight.
A real survivor, this small smoky backstreet *pivnice* is squeezed in between the embassies and still frequented mostly by Czechs.

Jo's Bar
Malostranské náměstí 7. Daily 11am–2am. The city's original American expat/backpacker hangout. It no longer has quite the same vitality but remains a good place to hook up with other travellers. There's also a club, *Jo's Garáž*, downstairs.

St Nicholas Café
Tržiště 10. Mon–Fri noon–1am, Sat & Sun 4pm–1am. Small vaulted cellar bar that pulls in well-dressed older Czechs and the expat diplomatic crowd for pizza and Pilsner.

U bílé kuželky (The White Bowling Pin)
Míšeňská 12. Daily noon–11pm. Not a bad pub considering its touristy location right by the Charles Bridge, with reasonably priced Pilsner Urquell, Czech pub food and the occasional accordionist.

U kocoura (The Cat)
Nerudova 2. Daily 11am–11pm. One of the few famous old pubs left on Nerudova, serving Budvar, plus the obvious Czech stomach-fillers.

Clubs and live music

Malostranská beseda
Malostranské náměstí 21. Daily 5–11pm. Live-music venue that attracts lots of Czechs, despite its location. The programme is a mixture of rock, roots and jazz.

U malého Glena (Little Glenn's)
Karmelitská 23 ⓦ www.malyglen.cz. Live music nightly 9.30pm–1am. The tiny downstairs stage is worth checking out for its eclectic mix of Latin jazz, bebop and blues.

PLACES Malá Strana

Staré Město

Staré Město – literally the "Old Town" – is Prague's most central, vital ingredient. The capital's busiest markets, shops, restaurants and pubs are in this area, and during the day a gaggle of shoppers and tourists fills its complex and utterly confusing web of narrow byways. Yet despite all the commercial activity, there are still plenty of residential streets, giving the area a lived-in feel that is rarely found in European city centres. At the heart of the district is the Old Town Square (Staroměstské náměstí), Prague's showpiece main square, easily the most magnificent in central Europe, and a great place to get your bearings before heading off into the labyrinthine backstreets.

Charles Bridge (Karlův most)

Bristling with statuary and crowded with people, the Charles Bridge is by far the city's most famous monument. Built in the fourteenth century by Charles IV, the bridge originally featured just a simple crucifix. The first sculpture wasn't added until 1683, when St John of Nepomuk appeared. His statue was such a propaganda success that the Catholic church authorities ordered another 21 to be erected between 1706 and 1714. Individually, only a few of the works are outstanding, but taken collectively, set against the backdrop of the Hrad, the effect is breathtaking.

The bridge is now one of the city's most popular places to hang out, day and night: the crush of sightseers never abates during the day, when the niches created by the bridge-piers are occupied by souvenir-hawkers and buskers, but at night things calm down a bit, and the views

▲ CHARLES BRIDGE

are, if anything, even more spectacular.

You can climb both of the bridge's mighty Gothic gateways. The western one contains an exhibition (April–Nov daily 10am–6pm; 50Kč) relaying the history of the towers, the bridge itself, and the story of St John of Nepomuk (who was thrown to his death from the bridge in 1393). The eastern one (daily: March 10am–6pm; April, May & Oct 10am–7pm; June–Sept 10am–10pm; Nov–Feb 10am–5pm; 60Kč) contains a small display of antique musical instruments; both allow you out onto their roofs for a bird's-eye view of the bridge.

Church of sv František z Assisi (St Francis of Assisi)

Built in the 1680s, the interior of this half-brick church is dominated by its huge dome, decorated with a vast fresco of *The Last Judgement* and rich marble furnishings. The **Galerie Křižovníků** (Tues–Sun 10am–1pm & 2–6pm; 40Kč), next door, houses the church treasury, which contains a stunning collection of silver and gold chalices, monstrances and reliquaries.

Church of sv Salvátor (St Saviour)

The facade of this church prickles with saintly statues which are lit up enticingly at night. Founded in 1593, it marks the beginning of the Jesuits' rise to power and is part of the Klementinum (see below). Like many Jesuit churches, its design copies that of the Gesù church in Rome; it's worth a quick look, if only for the frothy stucco plasterwork and delicate ironwork in its triple-naved interior.

Karlova

As the quickest route between the Charles Bridge and the Old Town Square, the narrow street of Karlova is usually packed with people, their attention divided between checking out the souvenir shops and not losing their way. With Europop blaring from several shops, jesters' hats and puppets in abundance, and a strip club for good measure, the whole atmosphere can be a bit oppressive in the height of summer, and is in many ways better savoured at night.

PLACES

▲ PUPPET MUSEUM, KARLOVA

Klementinum

Daily: Jan–March 10am–4pm; April–Oct 10am–8pm; Nov & Dec 10am–6pm. 190Kč. As they stroll down Karlova, few people notice the former Jesuit College on the north side of the street, which covers an area second in size only to the castle. The Habsburg family summoned the Jesuits to Prague in 1556 to help bolster the Catholic cause in Bohemia, and put them in charge of the entire education system until their demise in 1773. The complex now belongs to the university and houses, among other things, the National Library.

Aside from the ornate **Mirrored Chapel** (Zrcadlová kaple), which is open only for

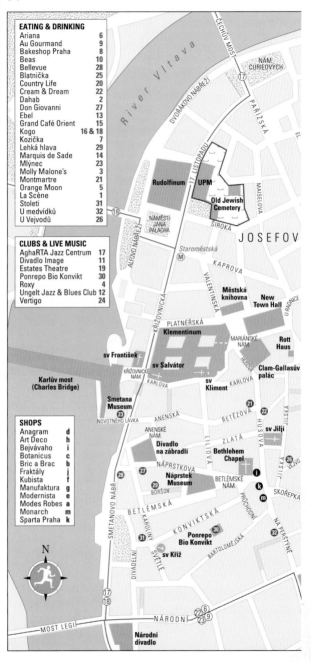

EATING & DRINKING

Ariana	6
Au Gourmand	9
Bakeshop Praha	8
Beas	10
Bellevue	28
Blatnička	25
Country Life	20
Cream & Dream	22
Dahab	2
Don Giovanni	27
Ebel	13
Grand Café Orient	15
Kogo	16 & 18
Kozička	7
Lehká hlava	29
Marquis de Sade	14
Mlýnec	23
Molly Malone's	3
Montmartre	21
Orange Moon	5
La Scène	1
Stoleti	31
U medvídků	32
U Vejvodů	26

CLUBS & LIVE MUSIC

AghaRTA Jazz Centrum	17
Divadlo Image	11
Estates Theatre	19
Ponrepo Bio Konvikt	30
Roxy	4
Ungelt Jazz & Blues Club	12
Vertigo	24

SHOPS

Anagram	d
Art Deco	h
Bejvávaho	i
Botanicus	c
Bric a Brac	b
Fraktály	j
Kubista	f
Manufaktura	g
Modernista	e
Modes Robes	a
Monarch	m
Sparta Praha	k

ČECHŮV MOST

NÁM.
CURIEOVÝCH

River Vltava

DVOŘÁKOVO NÁBŘEŽÍ

PAŘÍŽSKÁ

17. LISTOPADU

MAISELOVA

MÁNESŮV MOST

Rudolfinum   UPM

Old Jewish
Cemetery

NÁMĚSTÍ
JANA
PALACHA

ŠIROKÁ

JOSEFOV

ALŠOVO NÁBŘEŽÍ

Staroměstská

KAPROVA

VALENTINSKÁ

Městská
knihovna

New
Town Hall

U RADNICE

PLATNÉŘSKÁ

KŘIŽOVNICKÁ

Klementinum

MARIÁNSKÉ
NÁM.

HUSOVA

Rott
Haus

sv František

sv Salvátor

KŘIŽOVNICKÉ
NÁM.   KARLOVA

sv
Kliment   KARLOVÁ

Clam-Gallasův
palác

Karlův most
(Charles Bridge)

Smetana
Museum

NOVOTNÉHO LÁVKA

ANENSKÁ

ŘETĚZOVÁ

sv Jiljí

ANENSKÉ
NÁM.

ZLATÁ

Divadlo
na zábradlí

LILIOVÁ

Bethlehem
Chapel

VEJVODOVA

NÁPRSTKOVA

BORŠOV

Náprstek
Museum

BETLÉMSKÉ
NÁM.

PRŮCHODNÍ

SKOŘEPKA

SMETANOVO NÁBŘ.

BETLÉMSKÁ

KONVIKTSKÁ

KAROLINY

Ponrepo
Bio Konvikt

BARTOLOMĚJSKÁ

NA PERŠTYNĚ

DIVADELNÍ

SVĚTLÁ

sv Kříž

N

MOST LEGII

NÁRODNÍ

Národní
divadlo

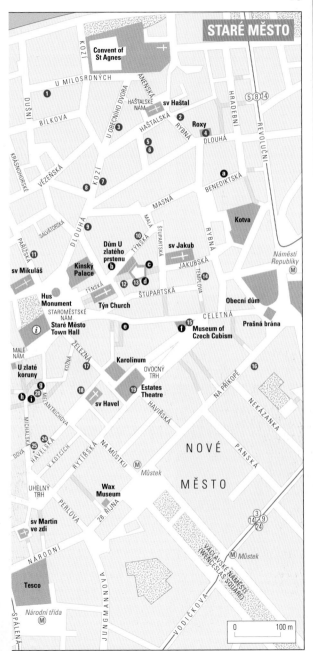

concerts, the Klementinum's most easily accessible attractions are now open to the public on a thirty-minute guided tour (in English). The most spectacular sight is the **Baroque Library**, a long room lined with leather tomes, whose ceiling is decorated by one continuous illusionistic fresco praising secular wisdom, and whose wrought-iron gallery balustrade is held up by wooden barley-sugar columns. Upstairs, at roughly the centre of the Klementinum complex, is the **Astronomical Tower**, from which you can enjoy a superb view over the centre of Prague.

New Town Hall (Nová radnice)

Mariánské náměstí 2 ⓦ www.praha-mesto.cz. The most striking features of the rather severe New Town Hall are the two gargantuan figures which stand guard at either corner. The one on the left, looking like Darth Vader, is the "Iron Knight", mascot of the armourers' guild;

▲ RABBI LÖW

to the right is the caricatured sixteenth-century Jewish sage and scholar, Rabbi Löw. According to legend, Löw was visited by Death on several occasions, but escaped his clutches until he reached the ripe old age of 97, when the Grim Reaper hid in a rose innocently given to him by his (in this case, naked) granddaughter.

Malé náměstí

A little cobbled square at the eastern end of Karlova, Malé náměstí was originally settled by French merchants in the twelfth century and is home to the city's first apothecary, **U zlaté koruny** (The Golden Crown), opened by a Florentine in 1353 at no. 13. The former pharmacy boasts chandeliers and a restored Baroque interior, though sadly it's now a jeweller's. The square's best-known building is the russet-red, neo-Renaissance **Rott Haus**, originally an ironmonger's shop founded by V.J. Rott in 1840, whose facade is smothered in agricultural scenes and motifs inspired by the Czech artist Mikuláš Aleš. At the centre of the square stands a (no longer functioning) fountain dating from 1560, which retains its beautiful, original wrought-iron canopy.

Staroměstské náměstí (Old Town Square)

Easily the most spectacular square in Prague, Staroměstské náměstí is the traditional heart of the city. Most of the brightly coloured houses look solidly eighteenth-century, but their Baroque facades hide considerably older buildings. Over the centuries, the square has seen its fair share of demonstrations and battles: the 27 white crosses set into the paving commemorate the Protestant leaders who were

▲ BAROQUE STATUE, OLD TOWN SQUARE

the panoramic view across Prague's spires. You can also visit the medieval chapel, which has patches of original wall painting, and wonderful grimacing corbels at the foot of the ribbed vaulting. If you get there just before the clock strikes the hour, you can also watch the Apostles going out on parade.

Astronomical Clock

Hourly 9am–9pm. The most popular feature on Staroměstské náměstí is the town hall's fifteenth-century Astronomical Clock, whose hourly mechanical dumbshow regularly attracts a crowd of tourists. Little figures of the Apostles shuffle past the top two windows, bowing to the audience, while perched on pinnacles below are the four threats to the city as perceived by the medieval mind: Death carrying his hourglass and tolling his bell, the Jew with his moneybags (since 1945 shorn

condemned to death on the orders of the Habsburg Emperor in 1621, while the patch of green grass marks the neo-Gothic east wing of the town hall, burned down by the Nazis on the final day of the Prague Uprising in May 1945. Nowadays, the square is filled with café tables in summer and an ice rink and Christmas market in winter, while tourists pour in all year round to watch the town hall's astronomical clock chime, to sit on the benches in front of the Hus Monument, and to drink in the atmosphere of this historic showpiece.

Staré Město Town Hall (Staroměstská radnice)

Mon 11am–6pm, Tues–Sun 9am–6pm, Nov–March closes 5pm. 60Kč. The Staré Město Town Hall occupies a whole sequence of houses on Staroměstské náměstí, culminating in an obligatory wedge-tower with a graceful Gothic oriel. It's hardly worth taking the twenty-minute guided tour of the few rooms that survived the last war, but it's fun to climb the tower for

▼ STARÉ MĚSTO TOWN HALL

▲ ASTRONOMICAL CLOCK

of his stereotypical beard and referred to as Greed), Vanity admiring his reflection, and a turbaned Turk shaking his head. Beneath the moving figures, four characters representing Philosophy, Religion, Astronomy and History stand motionless throughout the performance. Finally, a cockerel pops out and flaps its wings to signal that the show's over; the clock then chimes the hour.

Hus Monument

The colossal Jan Hus Monument, unveiled in 1915, features a turbulent sea of blackened bodies – the oppressed to his right, the defiant to his left – out of which rises the majestic moral authority of Hus himself, a radical religious reformer and martyr from the fifteenth century. The Austrians refused to hold an official unveiling of the statue; in protest, on the 500th anniversary of his death, Praguers smothered the monument in flowers. Since then it has been a powerful symbol of Czech nationalism: in March 1939, it was draped in swastikas by the invading Nazis, and in August 1968, it was shrouded in funereal black by Praguers, protesting at the Soviet invasion. The inscription along the base is a quote from the will of Comenius (see p.64), one of Hus's seventeenth-century followers, and includes Hus's most famous dictum, *Pravda vitězí* (Truth Prevails), which has been the motto of just about every Czech revolution since then.

Kinský Palace

Staroměstské náměstí 12 ⓦ www.ngprague.cz. Tues–Sun 10am–6pm. 100Kč. The largest secular building on the square is the Rococo Kinský Palace, which was once a German Gymnasium, attended by, among others, Franz Kafka (whose father ran a haberdashery shop on the ground floor). The palace is perhaps most notorious, however, as the venue for the fateful speech by the Communist prime minister, Klement Gottwald, who walked out onto the grey stone balcony one snowy February morning in 1948, flanked by his Party henchmen, to celebrate the Communist takeover with the thousands of enthusiastic supporters who packed the square below. Gottwald's appearance forms the memorable opening to Milan Kundera's novel *The Book of Laughter and Forgetting*. The top two floors currently house a vast permanent collection of Czech landscape paintings – hardly a popular subject, and a slightly perverse one given the gallery's prime location.

PLACES

Staré Město

Týn church (Chrám Matky boží před Týnem)

Celetná 5 ⊚tynska.farnost.cz. Mon–Fri 10am–1pm & 3–5pm. Free. The mighty Týn church is by far the most imposing Gothic structure in the Staré Město. Its two irregular towers, bristling with baubles, spires and pinnacles, rise like giant antennae above the arcaded houses which otherwise obscure its facade, and are spectacularly lit up at night. Inside, the church has a lofty, narrow nave punctuated at ground level by black and gold Baroque altarpieces. One or two original Gothic furnishings survive, most notably the pulpit and the fifteenth-century baldachin, housing a winged altar in the north aisle. Behind the pulpit, you'll find another superb winged altar depicting John the Baptist, dating from 1520. The pillar on the right of the chancel steps contains the red marble tomb of Tycho Brahe, the famous Danish astronomer who was court astronomer to Rudolf II.

▲ ARCADES IN TYN COURTYARD

Dům U zlatého prstenů (House of the Golden Ring)

Týnská 6 ⊚www.ghmp.cz. Tues–Sun 10am–6pm. 150Kč. Housed in a handsome Gothic town house, this art gallery offers a good taster of **twentieth-century Czech art**. The permanent collection is spread out over three floors, and arranged thematically rather than chronologically, while the cellars provide space for contemporary exhibitions; there's also a nice café across the courtyard. The pictures on display change quite frequently, but first-floor highlights should include *Destitute Land*, Max Švabinský's none-too-subtle view of life under the Habsburg yoke; works by two of Bohemia's best-loved eccentrics, Josef Váchal and František Bílek; and the odd Socialist Realist piece like Eduard Stavinoha's cartoon-like *Striking Demonstrators 24.2.1948*. The second floor ranges from Antonín Slavíček's easy-on-the-eye Impressionist views of Prague to dissident works such as Michael Rittstein's political allegory *Slumber beneath a Large Hand* and Eva Kmentová's plaster-cast *Hands* peppered with bullet holes. On the third floor there's usually an excellent collection of mad collages by Jiří Kolář, made up of cut-up pieces of reproductions of other artists' works.

Church of sv Jakub

Malá Štupartská 6. Mon–Sat 9.30am– noon & 2–4pm, Sun 2–4pm. Free. Before you enter the church make sure you admire the distinctive bubbling, stucco portal above the main entrance. The church's massive Gothic proportions – it has the longest nave in Prague after the cathedral – make it a favourite venue for organ recitals and other concerts. After the great fire of 1689, Prague's Baroque artists remodelled the entire interior, adding huge pilasters, a series of colourful frescoes and over twenty side altars. The church has close historical links with the butchers of Prague, who are responsible for the thoroughly decomposed human forearm hanging high up on the west wall, on the right as you enter. It has been there for over four hundred years now, ever since a thief tried to steal the jewels of the Madonna from the high altar. As the thief reached out, the Virgin supposedly grabbed his arm and refused to let go. The next day the congregation of butchers had no option but to lop it off, and it has hung there as a warning ever since.

Convent of St Agnes (Anežský klášter)

U milosrdných 17 ⓦ www.ngprague. cz. Tues–Sun 10am–6pm. 100Kč.
Prague's oldest surviving Gothic building, founded in 1233 as a Franciscan convent for the Order of the Poor Clares, now provides a fittingly atmospheric setting for the city's chief medieval art collection. The exhibition is arranged chronologically, starting with a remarkable silver-gilt casket from 1360 used to house the skull of St Ludmila. The nine panels from the Vyšší Brod altarpiece, from around 1350, are also among the finest in central Europe. The real gems of the collection, however, are the six panels by Master Theodoric, who painted over one hundred such paintings for Charles IV's castle chapel at Karlštejn. These larger-than-life, half-length portraits of saints, church fathers and so on are full of intense expression and richly coloured detail, their depictions spilling onto the embossed frames. For a glimpse of some extraordinary draughtsmanship, check out the woodcuts by the likes of Cranach the Elder and Dürer – the seven-headed beast in Dürer's Apocalypse cycle is particularly Harry Potter. As you exit, you get to see the inside of the Gothic cloisters and the bare church that serves as a resting place for, among others, Václav I (1205–53) and St Agnes herself.

▲ CONVENT OF ST AGNES

Museum of Czech Cubism (Muzeum českého kubismu)

Ovocný trh 19 ⓦ www.ngprague.cz. Tues–Sun 10am–6pm. 100Kč. The museum is housed in **Dům U černé Matky boží** (House at the Black Madonna), built as a department store in 1911–12 by Josef Gočár and one of the best examples of Czech Cubist architecture in Prague. The permanent collection on the top two floors has a little bit of everything that the short-lived Czech Cubist movement produced, from sofas and sideboards by Gočár himself to paintings by Emil Filla and Josef Čapek, plus some wonderful sculptures by Otto Gutfreund and models of the Cubist villas in Vyšehrad (see p.116).

Estates Theatre (Stavovské divadlo)

Ovocný trh 1. The lime-green and white Estates Theatre was built in the early 1780s for the entertainment of Prague's large and powerful German community and remains one of the finest Neoclassical buildings in Prague, reflecting the enormous self-confidence of its patrons. The theatre has a place in Czech history, too, however, for it was here that the Czech national anthem, "Kde domov můj" ("Where Is My Home"), was first performed. It is also something of a mecca for Mozart fans, since it was here that the premieres of *Don Giovanni* and *La Clemenza di Tito* took place. This is, in fact, one of the few opera houses in Europe which remains intact from Mozart's time (though it underwent major refurbishment during the nineteenth century), and it was used by Miloš Forman to film the concert scenes for his Oscar-laden *Amadeus*.

Wax Museum (Muzeum voskových figurín)

Melantrichova 5 ⓦ www. waxmuseumprague.cz. Daily 9am–8pm. 120Kč. For anyone familiar with London's is Madame Tussaud's, the formula of Prague's Wax Museum is predictable enough, though some of the Czech wax tableaux will remain slightly baffling unless you know your Czech history. The most popular section with the locals is the podium of Commie stooges ranging from Lenin to the Czechs' home-grown Stalinist, Klement Gottwald, followed by today's generation of Czech politicians dressed in bad suits.

Bethlehem Chapel (Betlémská kaple)

Betlémské náměstí 4. Tues–Sun: April–Oct 10am–6.30pm; Nov–March 10am–5.30pm. 40Kč. The Bethlehem Chapel was founded in 1391 by religious reformists, who, denied the right to build a church, proceeded instead to build the largest chapel in

▲ SCULPTURE, ESTATES THEATRE

PLACES · Staré Město

Bohemia, with a total capacity of exactly 3000. Sermons were delivered not in the customary Latin, but in the language of the masses – Czech. From 1402 to 1413, Jan Hus preached here, regularly pulling in more than enough commoners to fill the chapel, while the leader of the German Peasants' Revolt, Thomas Müntzer, also preached here in the sixteenth century. Of the original building, only the three outer walls remain, with restored patches of the biblical scenes which were used to get the message across to the illiterate congregation. The rest is a scrupulous reconstruction, using the original plans and a fair amount of imaginative guesswork.

Náprstek Museum

Betlémské náměstí 1 ⓦ www.aconet. cz/npm. Tues–Sun 10am–6pm. 80Kč. Vojta Náprstek, founder of the Náprstek Museum, was inspired by the great Victorian museums of London and turned the family brewery into a museum, initially intending it to concentrate on the virtues of industrial progress. Náprstek's interests gradually shifted towards anthropology, however, and it is his ethnographic collections from the Americas, Australasia and Oceania that are now displayed in the museum. Despite the fact that the museum could clearly do with an injection of cash, it still manages to put on some really excellent temporary ethnographic exhibitions on the ground floor, and also does a useful job of promoting tolerance of different cultures.

Smetana Museum

Novotného lávka 1 ⓦ www.nm.cz. Daily except Tues 10am–noon & 12.30–5pm. 50Kč. Housed in a gaily decorated neo-Renaissance building on the riverfront, the Smetana Museum celebrates the life and work of the most nationalist of all the great Czech composers. He enjoyed his greatest success as a composer with *The Bartered Bride*, which marked the birth of Czech opera, but he was forced to give up conducting in 1874 with the onset of deafness, and eventually died of syphilis in a mental asylum. Unfortunately, the museum fails to capture much of the spirit of the man, though the views across to the castle are good, and you get to wave a laser baton around in order to listen to his music.

Shops

Anagram

Týn 4 ⓦ www.anagram.cz. Mon–Sat 10am–8pm, Sun 10am–7pm. Superb English-language bookstore which has lots of books on Czech politics and culture, plus a small secondhand section.

Art Deco

Michalská 21. Mon–Fri 2–7pm. A stylish antique shop crammed with a wonderful mixture of clothes, hats, mufflers, teapots, glasses, clocks and art.

Bejvávaho

Jilská 22 & 7 ⓦ www.marionettes. cz. Daily 10am–8pm. Large shop with a really wide range of marionettes, rod and glove puppets.

Botanicus

Týn 3 ⓦ www.botanicus.cz. Daily 10am–6.30pm. Czech take on the UK's Body Shop, with a folksy ambience. Dried flowers and fancy honey are sold alongside natural soaps and shampoos.

▲ HAVELSKÁ MARKET

Bric a Brac

Týnská 7. Daily 10am–6pm. One of the best secondhand shops in central Prague, stuffed to the rafters with everything from antiques to clothes.

Fraktály

Betlémské náměstí 5. Mon–Sat 10am–8pm, Sun noon–8pm. Great bookshop with stylish armchairs to collapse into and peruse books on design, architecture and fine art, or a good place to pick up a groovy poster or arty gift.

Havelská market

Havelská. Mon–Fri 8am–6pm, Sat & Sun 9am–6pm. Open-air market that stretches the full length of the arcaded street of Havelská, selling fruit, flowers, vegetables, CDs, souvenirs and wooden toys.

Kubista

Ovocný trh 19 ⓦ www.kubista.cz. Tues–Sun 10am–6pm. Beautiful shop housed in the same building as the Museum of Czech Cubism and selling reproductions of some of the museum's exquisite Cubist ceramics.

Manufaktura

Melantrichova 17. Daily 10am–8pm. Czech folk-inspired shop with a fantastic array of wooden toys, painted Easter eggs, straw decorations, honeycomb candles and sundry kitchen utensils.

Modernista

Celetná 12 ⓦ www.modernista.cz. Daily 11am–7pm. Beautiful but pricey emporium selling top-drawer restored Czech furniture and furnishings in the functionalist style popular between the wars and beyond.

Modes Robes

Benediktská 5. Mon–Fri 10am–7pm, Sat 10am–4pm. Aladdin's cave women's boutique where you can sit down and have a coffee while trying on clothes by local designers.

Monarch

Na Perštýně 15. Mon–Sat noon–8pm. Emerging as the city's number one wine shop (and wine bar), with stock from all over the world as well as local wine – sells cheese and dried meats, too.

Sparta Praha

Betlémské náměstí 7. Mon–Thurs 10am–5pm, Fri 10am–4pm. Centrally located football fan shop stocking everything from soccer shirts to ashtrays, mostly for Sparta Praha, but also stocks Slavia Praha, Bohemians and Dukla Praha merchandise.

Cafés

Au Gourmand

Dlouhá 10. Daily 9am–7pm. Beautifully tiled French boulangerie, patisserie and traiteur selling wickedly delicious pastries; most folk take away, but there are a few tables and a daily soup on offer.

Bakeshop Praha

Kozí 1. Daily 7am–7pm. Top-class expat bakery serving excellent bread, sandwiches, quiches, wraps and cakes, which you can either take away or wash down with coffee whilst reading the papers.

Beas

Týnská 19. Mon–Sat 10am–8pm, Sun 10am–6pm. Bright, modern Indian veggie café through the courtyard off Týnská, offering simple, authentic dosas and thalis served on traditional metal trays.

Country Life

Melantrichova 15. Mon–Thurs 9am–8.30pm, Fri 9am–4pm, Sun 11am–8.30pm. Self-service café behind the health-food shop of the same name: pile up your plate with hot or cold dishes and salad and pay by weight.

Cream & Dream

Husova 12. Daily 11am–10pm. Multinational *gelateria* chain that serves up some of the best ice cream in Prague, with real fruit and no artificial rubbish.

Dahab

Dlouhá 33 ⓦ www.dahab.cz. Daily noon–1am. The mother of all Prague teahouses, a vast Bedouin tent of a place serving tasty Middle Eastern snacks, couscous and hookahs to a background of funky world music.

Ebel

Týn 2 ⓦ www.ebelcoffee.cz. Daily 9am–10pm. One of a fashionable chain of cafés serving very good coffee and tasty snacks, hidden away on the south side of the Týn (Ungelt) courtyard behind the Týn church.

Grand Café Orient

Ovocný trh 19. Daily 9am–9pm. Superb reconstruction of a famous Cubist café from 1911, on the first floor of the Museum of Czech Cubism, dishing up cakes, pancakes and coffee.

▲ STAROMĚTSKÉ NÁMĚSTÍ

Montmartre

Řetězová 7. Daily 8am–11pm. Surprisingly small, barrel-vaulted café that was once a famous First Republic dance and cabaret venue, frequented by the likes of Werfel, Jesenská and Hašek.

Restaurants

Ariana
Rámová 6 ☎ 222 323 438, Ⓦ www.
sweb.cz/kabulrest. Daily 11am–11pm.
Welcoming Afghan restaurant
serving up authentic spicy kebabs
and veggie dishes (150–250Kč) a
stone's throw from the Old Town
Square.

Bellevue
Smetanovo nábřeží 18 ☎ 222 221
438, Ⓦ www.bellevuerestaurant.cz.
Daily noon–3pm & 5.30–11pm. The
view of Charles Bridge and the
Hrad is outstanding, the setting is
very formal and the international
cuisine is imaginatively prepared
– hardly surprising, then, that
main courses are 500–800Kč and
you need to book ahead.

Don Giovanni
Karoliny Světlé 34 ☎ 222 222 060,
Ⓦ www.dongiovanni.cz. Daily 11am–
midnight. One of the best Italian
restaurants in town, with views
of Charles Bridge and a menu
offering all the classic dishes
(350–600Kč), plus fresh fish and
seafood and top-class tiramisu.

Kogo
Havelská 27 ☎ 224 214 543, Ⓦ www.
kogo.cz. Daily 9am–midnight.
Divided into two intimate spaces
by a passageway, and with a
small courtyard out back, this
place offers decent pasta, pizza
and salads for around 250Kč,
served by courteous and efficient
waiters.

La Scène
U milosrdných 6 ☎ 222 312 677,
Ⓦ www.lascene.cz. Daily 11am–2am.
Ultra-modern designer café-
restaurant offering salads and
brioches (95–125Kč) during the
day and Italian classics in the
evening including pasta (from

220Kč), fish dishes (from 400Kč)
and even marinated rabbit
(400Kč).

Lehká hlava (Clear Head)
Boršov 2 ☎ 222 220 665, Ⓦ www.
lehkahlava.cz. Daily 11.30am–
11.30pm. Exotic cave-like veggie
restaurant, just off Karoliny
Světlé, offering tapas, soups,
salads, pasta and quesadillas for
75–150Kč.

Mlýnec
Novotného lávka 9 ☎ 221 082 208,
Ⓦ www.mlynec.cz. Daily noon–3pm &
5.30–11pm. International cuisine
(which has occasionally garnered
Michelin stars) and a fabulous
terrace overlooking the Charles
Bridge and the Hrad. Mains
500–700Kč.

Orange Moon
Rámová 5 ☎ 222 325 119, Ⓦ www.
orangemoon.cz. Daily 11.30am–
11.30pm. Popular Burmese
restaurant that cooks up spicey
curries for under 200Kč, washed
down with Czech beer.

Stoleti
Karoliny Světlé 21 ☎ 222 220 008,
Ⓦ www.stoleti.cz. Daily noon–midnight.
Imaginative Czech cuisine named
after stars of film and stage served

▲ STOLETI RESTAURANT

PLACES

Staré Město

in an unstuffy, simply furnished restaurant. Mains around 200Kč.

Pubs and bars

Blatnička

Michalská 5. Mon–Fri 10am–9pm; wine bar daily 3pm–midnight. Wine shop where you can drink straight from the barrel, take away, or head next door to the popular basement vinárna for more wine and cheap Czech food.

Kozička

Kozí 4 ⓦ www.kozicka.cz. Mon–Fri noon–4am, Sat & Sun 6pm–4am. Busy, designer bare-brick cellar bar with cheap Czech food, tucked away just a short walk from Staroměstské náměstí.

Marquis de Sade

Templová 8. Daily 4pm–3am. Great space, with a huge high ceiling and big comfy sofas. Unfortunately, the beer's not great and it does attract a leery, mostly expat crowd.

Molly Malone's

U Obecního dvora 4 ⓦ www. mollymalones.cz. Mon–Thurs & Sun 11am–1am, Fri & Sat 11am–2am. The best of Prague's Irish pubs, with real Irish staff, an open fire, draught Kilkenny and Guinness, and decent Irish-themed food.

U medvídků (The Little Bears)

Na Perštýně 7. Mon–Sat 11.30am–11pm, Sun 11.30am–10pm. A Prague beer hall going back to the thirteenth century and still much the same as it always was (make sure you turn right when you enter, and avoid the new bar to the left). The Budvar comes

thick and fast, and the food is absolutely standard.

U zlatého tygra (The Golden Tiger)

Husava 17. Small central *pivnice* serving a very local loyal following; the late writer and bohemian, Bohumil Hrabal, was a semi-permanent resident.

U Vejvodů

Jilská 4 ⓦ www.restauraceuvejvodu.cz. Mon–Sat 10am–4am, Sun 11am–3am. This atmospheric beer hall is now one of Pilsner Urquell's very successful chain of pubs, serving poshed-up pub food.

Clubs, live music, film and performing arts

AghaRTA Jazz Centrum

Železná 16 ⓦ www.agharta.cz. Daily 7pm–1am. Probably the best jazz club in Prague, with a good mix of Czechs and foreigners and a consistently good programme of gigs.

Divadlo Image

Pařížská 4 ☏ 222 329 191, ⓦ www. imagetheatre.cz. One of the more innovative and entertaining of Prague's ubiquitous venues for "black light theatre" (visual trickery created by "invisible" actors dressed all in black).

Estates Theatre (Stavovské divadlo)

Ovocný trh 1 ☏ 224 901 448, ⓦ www. narodni-divadlo.cz. Prague's oldest opera house puts on a mixture of opera, ballet and straight theatre (with simultaneous headphone translation available).

Ponrepo Bio Konvikt

Bartolomějská 11 ☎ 224 237 233.
Really old classics from the
black-and-white era, dug out
from the National Film Archives.
You need to be a member to
visit; membership cards (150Kč)
can only be bought Mon–Fri
3–6pm (bring a passport photo).

Roxy

Dlouhá 33 ⓦ www.roxy.cz. Daily from
7pm. The centrally located *Roxy*
is a great little venue: a laid-back,
rambling old theatre with an
interesting programme of events
from arty films and exhibitions
to exceptional live acts and house
DJ nights.

Ungelt Jazz & Blues Club

Týn 2 ⓦ www.jazzblues.cz. Daily
7pm–2am. A good cellar venue
that pulls in lots of tourists due
to its central venue, but puts
on a decent selection of music
nevertheless, with the emphasis
on blues.

Vertigo

Havelská 9 ⓦ www.vertigo-club.cz.
Daily 9pm–4am. Very central club
with a decent dance floor and
sound system, and an eclectic rota
of themed nights.

PLACES

Staré Město

Josefov

The old Jewish ghetto district of Josefov is one of the most unforgettable sights in Prague. Although the warren-like street plan of the old ghetto was demolished in the 1890s to make way for streets of luxurious five-storey mansions, six synagogues, the Jewish town hall and the medieval cemetery still survive. There's no denying that the sheer volume of tourists visiting Josefov has turned the area into something of a tourist trap. Yet to skip this part of the old town is to miss out on a fascinating and essential slice of the city's cultural history.

Franz Kafka Museum

U radnice 5. Tues–Fri 10am–6pm, Sat 10am–5pm. 50Kč. The writer Franz Kafka was born on July 3, 1883, above the Batalion Schnapps bar on the corner of Maiselova and Kaprova. The original building

▲ FRANZ KAFKA

has long since been torn down, but a gaunt-looking modern bust now commemorates the site, next to which is the Frank Kafka Museum, a modest exhibition retelling Kafka's life simply but effectively with pictures and quotes. Kafka spent most of his life living in and around Josefov, working as an accident insurance clerk, until he was forced to retire through ill health in 1922. He died of tuberculosis in a sanatorium just outside Vienna, on June 3, 1924, and is buried in the New Jewish Cemetery in Žižkov (see p.118).

Old-New Synagogue (Staronová synagoga)

Červená 2. Begun in the second half of the thirteenth century, this is the oldest functioning synagogue in Europe, one of the earliest Gothic buildings in Prague and still the religious centre for Prague's Orthodox Jews. The simple, plain interior

All the major sights of Josefov (ⓦ www.jewishmuseum.cz) – the Old-New Synagogue, Old Jewish Cemetery, the Ceremonial Hall, the Maisl, Pinkas, Klaus and Spanish synagogues – are covered by an all-in-one ticket, available from any of the quarter's numerous ticket offices. This costs either 470Kč including the Old-New Synagogue, or 290Kč without. Opening hours vary but are basically daily except Saturday April–October 9am–6pm and November–March 9am–4.30pm.

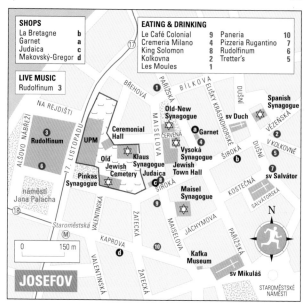

is mostly taken up with the elaborate wrought-iron cage enclosing the bimah in the centre. The tattered red standard on display was originally a gift to the community from Emperor Ferdinand II for helping fend off the Swedes in 1648.

Maisel, minister of finance to Rudolf II, in the sixteenth century, it was later rebuilt as the creamy-pink Baroque house you now see, housing, among other things, a kosher restaurant. The

▲ OLD-NEW SYNAGOGUE

Jewish Town Hall (Židovská radnice)

Maiselova 18. Not open to the public.
The Jewish Town Hall is one of the few such buildings in central Europe to survive the Holocaust. Founded and funded by Mordecai

▲ JEWISH TOWN HALL

belfry has a clock on each of its four sides, plus a Hebrew one stuck on the north gable which, like the Hebrew script, goes "backwards".

Maisel Synagogue

Maiselova 10. Like the town hall, the neo-Gothic Maisel Synagogue was founded and paid for entirely by Mordecai Maisel. Set back from the neighbouring houses south down Maiselova, the synagogue was, in its day, one of the most ornate in Josefov. Nowadays, its bare whitewashed turn-of-the-century interior houses an exhibition on the history of the Jewish community up until the 1848 emancipation, as well as glass cabinets filled with gold and silverwork, Hanukkah candlesticks, Torah scrolls and other religious artefacts.

Pinkas Synagogue

Široká 3. Built in the 1530s for the powerful Horovitz family, the Pinkas Synagogue has undergone countless restorations over the centuries. In 1958, the synagogue was transformed into a chilling memorial to the 77,297 Czech Jews killed during the Holocaust. The memorial was closed shortly after the 1967 Six Day War – due to damp, according to the Communists – and remained so, allegedly due to problems with the masonry, until it was finally, painstakingly restored in the 1990s. All that remains of the synagogue's original decor today is the ornate bimah surrounded

by a beautiful wrought-iron grille, supported by barley-sugar columns.

Of all the sights of the Jewish quarter, the Holocaust memorial is perhaps the most moving, with every bit of wall space taken up with the carved stone list of victims, stating simply their name, date of birth and date of death or transportation to the camps. It is the longest epitaph in the world, yet it represents a mere fraction of those who died in the Nazi concentration camps. Upstairs in a room beside the women's gallery, there's also a harrowing exhibition of drawings by children from the Jewish ghetto in Terezín, most of whom were killed in the camps.

Old Jewish Cemetery (Starý židovský hřbitov)

Široká 3. At the heart of Josefov is the Old Jewish Cemetery, known as *beit hayyim* in Hebrew, meaning "House of Life". Established in the fifteenth century, it was in use until 1787, by which time there were an estimated 100,000 people buried here, one on top of the other, six palms apart, and as many as twelve layers deep. The enormous number of visitors has meant that the graves themselves have been roped off

▲ OLD JEWISH CEMETERY

The Holocaust

Under the Nazis, the majority of Prague's Jews were sent to their deaths, but, by a grotesque twist of fate, Josefov's synagogues, town hall and cemetery were preserved on Hitler's orders to form the centrepiece of his planned "Exotic Museum of an Extinct Race". To this end, Jewish artefacts from all over central Europe were gathered here by the Nazis, and today make up one of the most comprehensive collections of Judaica in Europe.

to protect them, and a one-way system introduced: you enter from the Pinkas Synagogue and leave by the Klaus Synagogue. Get there before the crowds – a difficult task for much of the year – and the cemetery can be a poignant reminder of the ghetto, its inhabitants subjected to inhuman overcrowding even in death. The rest of Prague recedes beyond the sombre lime trees and cramped perimeter walls, the haphazard headstones and Hebrew inscriptions casting a powerful spell. On many graves you'll see pebbles, some holding down *kvitlech* or small messages of supplication.

Ceremonial Hall (Obřadní síň)

U starého hřbitova. Immediately on your left as you leave the cemetery is the Ceremonial Hall, a lugubrious neo-Renaissance house built in 1906 as a ceremonial hall by the Jewish Burial Society. Appropriately enough, it's now devoted to an exhibition on Jewish traditions of burial and death, though it would probably be more useful if you could visit it before heading into the cemetery, rather than after.

Klaus Synagogue

U starého hřbitova 1. A late seventeenth-century building, the Klaus Synagogue was founded in the 1690s by Mordecai Maisel on the site of several small buildings (Klausen), in what was then a notorious red-light district of Josefov. The ornate Baroque interior contains a rich display of religious objects from embroidered *kippah* to Kiddush cups, and explains the very basics of Jewish religious practice, and the chief festivals or High Holidays.

Pařížská

Running through the heart of the old ghetto is Pařížská, the ultimate bourgeois avenue, lined with buildings covered in a riot of turn-of-the-century sculpturing, spikes and turrets. Totally at odds with the rest of Josefov, its ground-floor premises are home to designer clothes shops, jewellery stores and swanky cafés, restaurants and bars.

Spanish Synagogue

Vězeňská 1. Begun in 1868, the Spanish Synagogue is by far the most ornate synagogue in Josefov, its stunning, gilded Moorish interior deliberately imitating the Alhambra (hence its name). Every available surface is smothered with a profusion of floral motifs and geometric patterns, in vibrant reds, greens and blues, which are repeated in the synagogue's huge stained-glass windows. The synagogue also houses an interesting exhibition on the history of Prague's Jews from the time of the 1848 emancipation to the Holocaust. Lovely, slender, painted cast-iron columns hold

▲ SPANISH SYNAGOGUE

UPM (Museum of Decorative Arts)

17 listopadu 2 ⓦ www.upm.cz. Tues–Sun 10am–6pm. 120Kč. From its foundation in 1885 through to the end of the First Republic, the Uměleckoprůmyslové muzeum or UPM received the best that the Czech modern movement had to offer – from Art Nouveau to the avant-garde – and its collection is consequently unrivalled. The building itself is richly decorated in mosaics, stained glass and sculptures, and its ground-floor temporary exhibitions are consistently excellent. The permanent collection begins on the first floor with the Votive Hall, which is ornately decorated with trompe l'oeil wall hangings, lunette paintings and a bewhiskered bust of Emperor Franz-Josef I. Next door is the "Story of a Fibre", which is dominated by a double-decker costume display: richly embroidered religious vestments above and fashionable attire from the eighteenth century to modern catwalk concoctions below.

The "Arts of Fire" is home to the museum's impressive glass, ceramic and pottery displays, from eighteenth-century Meissen figures to Art-Nouveau Lötz vases. The print and images room is devoted mainly to Czech photography, and includes numerous prints from the art form's interwar heyday, including several works by František Drtikol, Jaromír Funkes and Josef Sudek. Finally, in the treasure hall, there's a kind of modern-day Kunstkammer or cabinet of curiosities: everything from ivory objets d'art and seventeenth-century Italian *pietre dure* (hardstone mosaics) to miniature silver furniture and a goblet made from rhino horn.

up the women's gallery, where the displays include a fascinating set of photos depicting the old ghetto at the time of its demolition. There's a section on Prague's German-Jewish writers, including Kafka, and information on the Holocaust.

Rudolfinum

Alšovo nábřeží 12. Tues–Sun 10am–6pm. The Rudolfinum, or House of Artists (Dům umělců), is one of the proud civic buildings of the nineteenth-century Czech national revival. Originally built to house an art gallery, museum and concert hall for the Czech-speaking community, it became the seat of the new Czechoslovak parliament, until 1938 when it was closed down by the Nazis. Since 1946, the building has returned to its original artistic purpose and it's now one of the capital's main concert venues (home to the Czech Philharmonic) and exhibition spaces.

93

Shops

Garnet

Pařížská 20. Daily 10am–6pm. The best place to get hold of fiery red Bohemian garnets or Polish amber jewellery.

Judaica

Široká 7. Mon–Fri 10am–6pm, Sun 10am–4pm. Probably the best-stocked of all the places flogging Jewish books to passing tourists, with books and prints, secondhand and new.

La Bretagne

Široká 22. Mon–Sat 9.30am–7.30pm. There's a wide array of fresh fish and seafood at this centrally located fishmonger's, plus takeaway sushi.

Makovský-Gregor

Kaprova 9. Mon–Fri 9am–7pm, Sat & Sun 10am–6pm. Appealingly chaotic little secondhand bookshop with old prints and English-language books.

Cafés

Cremeria Milano

Pařížská 20. Daily 9am–11pm. Really swanky Italian-style *gelateria* that serves up Cream & Dream ice cream; eat in or take-away.

Nostress

Dušní 10. Daily 10am–midnight. Despite the naff name, this smart, Belgian-owned café is actually a great place in which to unwind amidst the eclectic designer furniture. Decent salads and snacks on offer too.

Paneria

Kaprova 3. Daily 8am–8pm. Central branch of a large chain of Czech bakeries specializing in providing sandwiches, toasted panini and pastries.

Rudolfinum

Alšovo nábřeží 12. Tues–Sun 10am–6pm. Gloriously grand nineteenth-century café on the first floor of the old parliament building – you don't have to visit the gallery to go to the café.

▲ PARIZSKA PRAGUE

Restaurants

Le Café Colonial

Široká 6 ☎ 224 818 322, ⊛ www. lecafecolonial.cz. Daily 10am–midnight. Conveniently situated informal café/formal restaurant right opposite the Klausová synagoga. The colonial theme isn't overplayed, though the vast French-based menu has a touch of Chinese and Indian. Main courses around 400Kč.

King Solomon

Široká 8 ☎224 818 752, ⓦwww. kosher.cz. Daily 11am–11pm except Fri when it closes 1hr 30min before dusk. Prague's only certified kosher restaurant is a sophisticated place which serves big helpings of international dishes and traditional Jewish fare: a three-course set menu will set you back 550Kč.

Les Moules

Pařížská 19 ☎222 315 022, ⓦwww. lesmoules.cz. Daily 11.30am–midnight. Part of a chain of wood-panelled Belgian brasseries which flies in fresh mussels and serves them up for around 450Kč, with French fries and Belgian beers.

Pizzeria Rugantino

Dušní 4 ☎222 318 172, ⓦwww. rugantino.cz. Mon–Sat 11am–11pm, Sun noon–11pm. This pizzeria, just off Dlouhá, is the genuine article: an oak-fired oven, gargantuan thin bases and numerous toppings to choose from (140–210Kč).

Pravda (Truth)

Pařížská 17 ☎222 326 203. Daily noon–1am. Trendy restaurant on Prague's premier chic street pulling in fashionable customers. Service is attentive and the excellent menu ranges from Cajun to Vietnamese, with home-made pasta dishes around 360Kč and main dishes starting at around 600Kč.

Pubs

Kolkovna

V kolkovně 8. Daily 11am–midnight. Justifiably popular place with plush pub decor, excellent pub food and Pilsner Urquell on tap.

Tretter's

V kolkovně 3 ⓦwww.tretters.cz. Daily 7pm–3am. Wonderfully smart and sophisticated (but not exclusive) American cocktail bar, with very professional staff and a celebrity air about the place.

Live music

Rudolfinum

Alšovo nábřeží 12 ☎227 059 352, ⓦwww.rudolfinum.cz. A truly stunning neo-Renaissance concert hall from the late nineteenth century that's home base for the Czech Philharmonic.

Wenceslas Square and northern Nové Město

Nové Město – Prague's "New Town" – is the city's main commercial and business district, housing most of its big hotels, cinemas, nightclubs, fast-food outlets and department stores. Architecturally, it comes over as big, bourgeois and predominantly turn-of-the-century, yet the large market squares and wide streets were actually laid out way back in the fourteenth century by Emperor Charles IV. The obvious starting point in Nové Město is Wenceslas Square (Václavské náměstí), the long, sloping boulevard with its distinctive, interwar shopping malls, which was at the centre of the 1989 demonstrations against communism and is today at the hub of the modern city.

Wenceslas Square (Václavské náměstí)

The natural pivot around which modern Prague revolves, Wenceslas Square is more of a wide, gently sloping boulevard than a square as such. It's scarcely a conventional – or even convenient – space in which to hold mass demonstrations, yet for the last hundred and fifty years or more it has been the focus of political protest in Prague. In August 1968, it was the scene of some of the most violent confrontations between the Soviet invaders and the local Czechs, and it was at the top of the square, on January 16, 1969, that **Jan Palach** set fire to himself in protest at the continuing occupation of the country by Russian troops. More happily, in late November 1989, more than 250,000 people crammed into the square night after night, often enduring subzero temperatures, to demand free elections.

Despite the square's medieval origins, it is now lined with self-important six- or seven-storey buildings representing every artistic trend of the last hundred years, from neo-Renaissance to Socialist Realism. At the top of the

Prague's pasáže

Wenceslas Square has an impressive array of old shopping arcades, or *pasáže*, as they're known in Czech, dating from the interwar period. Compared with the chic passages off the Champs Elysées, Prague's *pasáže* offer more modest pleasures: a few shops, the odd café and, more often than not, a cinema. The king of the lot is the lavishly decorated Lucerna *pasáž*, stretching all the way from Štěpánská to Vodičkova, and boasting an equally ornate cinema, café and vast concert hall.

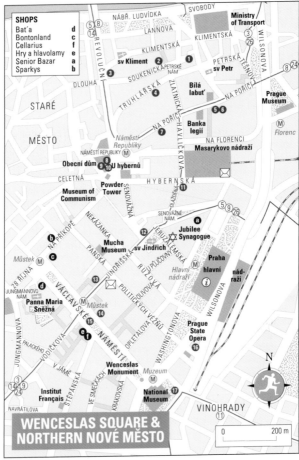

WENCESLAS SQUARE & NORTHERN NOVÉ MĚSTO

EATING & DRINKING		Grand Hotel Evropa	14	CLUBS & VENUES	
Albio	4	Modrý Zub	13	Divadlo Archa	6
American Bar	10	Plzeňská restaurace	8	Obecní dům	9
Archa	5	Tramvaj	15	Prague State Opera	16
Arco	11	U Góvindy	2		
Červená Tabulka	1	U sádlů	3		
Dinitz	7	Zahrada v opéře	17		
Francouzská restaurace	8	Zvonice	12		

square, in front of the grandiose National Museum, stands the **Wenceslas Monument**, a worthy and heroic, but pretty unexciting, equestrian statue of the country's patron saint. Below the statue, a simple memorial commemorating the victims of communism is adorned with flowers and photos of Jan Palach and Jan Zajíc, both of whom martyred themselves

▲ WENCESLAS MONUMENT

here in 1969 in protest at the Soviet invasion.

National Museum (Národní muzeum)

Václavské náměstí 68 ⓦ www.nm.cz. Daily: May–Sept 10am–6pm; Oct–April 9am–5pm. 110Kč. Deliberately modelled on the great European museums of Paris and Vienna, the broad, brooding hulk of the National Museum, built in 1890, dominates the view up the square like a giant golden eagle with outstretched wings. One of the great landmarks of the nineteenth-century Czech national revival, the museum is old-fashioned and underfunded, but it's worth taking at least a quick look at the ornate marble entrance hall and splendid monumental staircase leading to the glass-domed Pantheon, with its 48 busts and statues of distinguished bewhiskered Czech men (plus a couple of token women and Slovaks). The rest of the permanent collection is dowdy, poorly labelled and filled with coins, fossils and stuffed animals. The museum's temporary exhibitions can be very good, however, so it's always worth checking to see what's on.

Na příkopě

Na příkopě (literally "On the Moat") traces the course of the old moat, which was finally paved over in 1760. The street still marks the border between Staré Město and Nové Město, with the dividing line running down the middle of the street. At the turn of the century, these two partly pedestrianized streets formed the chief venue for the weekend passeggiata, and even today they are among the most crowded expanses of pavement in Prague. Along with a variety of swanky stores, banks, restaurants and clubs, you'll also discover some of the city's most ostentatious late nineteenth- and early twentieth-century buildings.

▲ KIOSK, WENCESLAS SQUARE

Museum of Communism

Na příkopě 10 ⓦ www. muzeumkomunismu.cz. Daily 9am–9pm. 180Kč. Above a casino, on the first floor of the Savarin Palace, the Museum of Communism gives a brief rundown of Czech twentieth-century history, accompanied by a superb collection of Communist statues, film footage and propaganda posters. The politics are a bit simplistic – the popular postwar support for the Party is underplayed – but it's worth tracking down for the memorabilia alone. Wrangles with the landlord may mean the place has to move premises, so check the website before visiting.

Powder Tower (Prašná brána)

Daily: April–Oct 10am–6pm. 50Kč. One of the eight medieval gate-towers that once guarded Staré Město, the Powder Tower was begun by King Vladislav Jagiello in 1475, shortly after he'd moved into the royal court, which was situated next door at the time. Work stopped when he retreated to the Hrad to avoid the wrath of his subjects; later on, it was used to store gunpowder – hence the name and the reason for the damage incurred in 1757, when it blew up. The small historical exhibition inside traces the tower's architectural metamorphosis over the centuries, up to its present remodelling in the nineteenth century. Most people, though, ignore the displays, and climb straight up for the modest view from the top.

Obecní dům (Municipal House)

Náměstí Republiky 5 ⓦ www.obecni-dum.cz. Attached to the Powder Tower, and built on the ruins of the old royal court, the Obecní dům is by far the most exciting Art Nouveau building in Prague, one of the few places that still manages to conjure up the atmosphere of Prague's turn-of-the-century café society.

Conceived as a cultural centre for the Czech community, it's probably the finest architectural achievement of the Czech national revival, extravagantly decorated inside and out by the leading Czech artists of the day. From the lifts to the cloakrooms, just about all the furnishings remain as they were when the building was completed in 1911.

The simplest way of soaking up the interior – peppered with mosaics and pendulous brass chandeliers – is to have a coffee in the cavernous café (see p.101). For a more detailed inspection of the building's spectacular interior, you can sign up for one of the regular guided tours at the information centre (daily 10am–6pm; 150Kč) on the ground floor.

Jubilee Synagogue

Jeruzalémská. Mid-April to Oct daily except Sat 1–5pm. 50Kč. Named in honour of the sixtieth year of the Emperor Franz-Josef I's reign in 1908, the Jubilee Synagogue was built in an incredibly colourful Moorish style similar to that of the Spanish Synagogue in Josefov, but with a touch of Art Nouveau. The Hebrew quote from Malachi on the facade strikes a note of liberal optimism: "Do we not have one father? Were we not created by the same God?"

Mucha Museum

Panská 7 ⓦ www.mucha.cz. Daily 10am–6pm. 120Kč. Dedicated to Alfons Mucha (1860–1939), probably the most famous of all Czech artists in the West, this museum has proved very popular. Mucha made his name in *fin-de-siècle* Paris, where he shot to fame after designing Art Nouveau posters for the actress Sarah Bernhardt. "Le Style Mucha" became all the rage, but the artist himself came to despise this "commercial" period of his work, and, in 1910, Mucha moved back to his homeland and threw himself into the national cause, designing patriotic stamps, banknotes and posters for the new republic. The whole of Mucha's career is covered in the permanent exhibition, and an excellent video (in English) covers the decade of his life he devoted to the cycle of nationalist paintings known as the Slav Epic. In the end, Mucha paid for his Czech nationalism with his life; dragged in for questioning by the Gestapo after the 1939 Nazi invasion, he died shortly after being released.

Praha hlavní nádraží (Prague Main Train Station)

▲ PRAHA HLAVNI NÁDRAŽÍ

Prague's main railway station is one of the final architectural glories of the dying Habsburg Empire, designed by Josef Fanta and officially opened in 1909 as the Franz-Josefs Bahnhof. Arriving by metro, or buying tickets in the over-polished subterranean modern section, it's easy to miss the station's surviving Art Nouveau parts. The original entrance on busy Wilsonova still exudes imperial confidence, with its wrought-iron canopy and naked figurines clinging to the sides of the towers. You can sit and admire the main foyer from the café, *Fantová kavárna* (daily 6am–11pm) – it's also worth heading north from the foyer to take a peek at the ceramic pillars in the former station restaurant.

Banka legií

Na poříčí 24. Mon–Fri 9am–5pm. Free. The Banka legií (now a branch of the ČSOB) is one of Prague's most unusual pieces of corporate architecture. A Rondo-Cubist building from the early 1920s, it boasts a striking white marble frieze by Otto Gutfreund, depicting the epic march across Siberia undertaken by the Czechoslovak Legion and their embroilment in the Russian Revolution, set into the bold smoky-red moulding of the facade. You're free to wander into the main banking hall on the ground floor, which, though marred by the current bank fittings, retains its curved glass roof and distinctive red-and-white marble patterning. The glass-curtain-walled Bílá labut´ (White Swan) department store, opposite, is a good example of the functionalist style which was embraced in the late 1920s and 1930s.

Prague Museum

Na poříčí 52 ⓦ www.muzeumprahy. cz. Tues–Sun 9am–6pm. 80Kč. A purpose-built neo-Renaissance mansion next to a noisy motorway houses the Prague Museum. Inside, there's an ad hoc collection of the city's art, a number of antique bicycles, and usually an intriguing temporary exhibition on some aspect of the city. The museum's prize possession, though, is Antonín Langweil's paper model of Prague which he completed in the 1830s. It's a fascinating insight into early nineteenth-century Prague – predominantly Baroque, with the cathedral incomplete and the Jewish quarter "unsanitized" – and, consequently, has served as one of the most useful records for the city's restorers. The most surprising thing, of course, is that so little has changed.

Shops

Bontonland
Václavské náměstí 1 ⓦwww. bontonland.cz. Mon–Sat 8am–8pm, Sun 10am–7pm. In the *pasáž* at the bottom of Wenceslas Square, Prague's biggest record store, stocking rock, folk, jazz and classical, with headphones for previews to boot.

Baťa
Václavské náměstí 6. Mon–Fri 9am–8pm, Sat 10am–8pm, Sun 11am–7pm. Functionalist flagship store of Baťa shoe empire with five floors of fancy footwear in a prime position on Wenceslas Square.

Cellarius
Lucerna pasáž, Štěpánská 61 ⓦwww. cellarius.cz. Mon–Sat 9.30am–9pm, Sun 3–8pm. Very well-stocked shop in the Lucerna *pasáž*, where you can taste and take away Czech wines.

Hry a hlavolamy
Václavské naměstí 38. Mon–Fri 10am–7pm, Sat & Sun 11am–6pm. A small shop inside the Rokoko *pasáž* which stocks some great wooden puzzles and

brainteasers (*hlavolamy*), plus board games.

Senior Bazar
Senovážné náměstí 18. Mon–Fri 9am–5pm. One of the city's more stylish secondhand/retro clothes shops.

Sparkys
Na příkopě 22. Mon–Sat 10am–7pm, Sun 10am–6pm. Prague's top dům hraček (House of Toys) on four floors, which stocks everything from high-tech to traditional wooden toys.

▲ BÍLÁ LABUT DEPARTMENT STORE

Cafés

Albio
Truhlářská 18–20. Mon–Fri 11am–7pm, Sat 10am–5pm. Prague's most committed organic vegetarian/vegan café (at the back of the

▲ LUCERNA PASSAGE, WENCESLAS SQUARE

101

deli/bakery) serves a whole range of healthy dishes from wholewheat pasta and noodles to filled baguettes and (vegetarians be warned) fish.

Archa
Na poříčí 26. Mon–Fri 9am–10.30pm, Sat 10am–10pm, Sun noon–10pm. Designer café belonging to the avant-garde venue of the same name, with big fishbowl windows for people-watching.

Arco
Hybernská/Dlažděná. Mon–Fri 3–9.30pm. Busy after-work café that's a modern reconstruction of the Kaffeehaus that was once the haunt of Prague's German-speaking literati (including Kafka).

Dobrá čajovna
Václavské náměstí 14 www.tea. cz. Mon–Fri noon–9.30pm, Sat & Sun 3–9.30pm. Mellow, rarefied teahouse, with an astonishing variety of teas (and a few Middle Eastern snacks) served by waiters who slip by silently in their sandals.

Grand Hotel Evropa
Václavské náměstí 25. Daily 9.30am–11pm. This sumptuous Art Nouveau café has all its original fittings, but has reached a new low in ambience and service. For architectural curiosity only.

Obecní dům
Náměstí Republiky 5. Daily 7.30am–11pm. The vast *kavárna* (café), with its famous fountain, is in the more restrained south hall of this huge Art Nouveau complex, and has recently been glitteringly restored – an absolute aesthetic treat.

Tramvaj
Václavské náměstí. Mon–Sat 9am–midnight, Sun 10am–midnight. Two vintage no. 11 trams stranded in the middle of Wenceslas Square (where they used to run) have been converted into a café – a convenient spot for coffee, and easy to locate.

U Góvindy
Soukenická 27. Mon–Sat 11am–5.30pm. Daytime Hare Krishna (Haré Kršna in Czech) restaurant serving organic Indian veggie dishes at knock-down prices.

Restaurants

Červená tabulka (Red Tablet)
Lodecká 4 ☎ 224 810 401, www.cervenatabulka.cz. Daily 11.30am–11pm. Famed for its duck in gingerbread sauce and its wide choice of fish and seafood, this little villa restaurant delivers attentive service and has a slightly offbeat, cosy interior. Mains 250–450Kč.

Francouzská restaurace
Obecní dům, Náměstí Republiky 5 ☎ 222 002 770, www.obecni-dum.cz. Daily noon–3pm & 6–11pm. The Art Nouveau decor in this cavernous Obecní dům restaurant is absolutely stunning, though the service is over-formal and the French-style main dishes are a hefty 700–900Kč.

Modrý zub (Blue Tooth)
Jindřišská 5 ☎ 222 212 622. Daily 11am–11pm. Inexpensive Thai rice and noodle dishes (130–150Kč) in a place that has a modern wine-bar feel to it.

Plzeňská restaurace
Obecní dům, Náměstí Republiky 5 ☎ 222 002 770, www.obecni-dum.cz. Daily 11am–11pm. Decent Czech pub-restaurant in the cellar of the Obecní dům, cheaper than

the *Francouzská restaurace* upstairs, with main dishes from 300Kč, but not quite the same aesthetic experience.

U sádlů (The Lard)
Klimentská @www.usadlu.cz. Daily 11am–11.30pm. Deliberately over-the-top themed medieval banqueting hall serving inexpensive hearty fare (150–250Kč) and lashings of frothing Budvar.

Zahrada v opeře (Opera Garden)
Legerova 75 ☎224 239 685, @www. zahradavopere.cz. Daily 11.30am–1am. Striking modern interior and beautifully presented food from around the world at democratic prices (main dishes for 200–400Kč).

Zvonice (Belltower)
Jindřišská věž, Jindřišská ☎224 220 028, @www.restaurantzvonice. cz. Daily 11.30am–midnight. Atmospheric restaurant on the sixth and seventh floors of a medieval belltower. Lunch menu for 300Kč; traditional Czech main dishes in the evening start at around 500Kč.

Pubs and bars

American Bar
Obecní dům, Náměstí Republiky 5. Daily 11am–11pm. This 1910 bar in the basement of the Obecní dům has been restored to its former glamour.

Dinitz
Na příkopě 12 @www.dinitz.cz. Mon–Sat 11am–11pm. Cool, Deco-ish café-bar with live music every Friday, decent food and a good selection of cocktails.

Performing arts and film

Divadlo Archa
Na poříčí 26 ☎221 716 333, @www. archatheatre.cz. By far the most innovative venue in Prague, with two very versatile spaces, an art gallery and a café. The programming includes music, dance and theatre with an emphasis on the avant-garde. English subtitles or translation often available.

Obecní dům – Smetanova síň
Náměstí Republiky 5 ☎222 002 105, @www.obecni-dum.cz. Fantastically ornate Art Nouveau concert hall which usually kicks off the Prague Spring festival and is home to the excellent Prague Symphony Orchestra.

Prague State Opera (Státní opera Praha)
Wilsonova 4 ☎224 227 266, @www.opera.cz. A sumptuous nineteenth-century opera house, originally built by the city's German-speaking community. It's now the number-two venue for opera, with a repertoire that tends to focus on Italian works.

Národní and southern Nové Město

Off the conventional tourist trail, and boasting only a few minor sights, the network of cobbled streets immediately to the south of Národní is nevertheless great to explore, as it harbours a whole range of interesting cafés, pubs, restaurants and shops that have steadily colonised the area over the last decade or so. Southern Nové Město also boasts the city's finest stretch of waterfront, with a couple of leafy islands overlooked by magnificent fin-de-siècle mansions that continue almost without interruption south to Vyšehrad.

Jungmannovo náměstí

Jungmannovo náměstí is named for Josef Jungmann (1772–1847), a prolific writer, translator and leading light of the Czech national revival, whose pensive, seated statue surveys the small, ill-proportioned square. The square itself boasts a couple of Czech architectural curiosities, starting with a unique **Cubist streetlamp** from 1912, beyond the Jungmann statue in the far eastern corner. The square's most imposing building is the chunky, vigorously sculptured **Palác Adria**, designed in Rondo-Cubist style in the early 1920s, with sculptural extras by Otto Gutfreund. The building's *pasáž* (arcade) still retains its wonderful original portal featuring sculptures depicting the twelve signs of the zodiac. The theatre in the basement was once a studio for the multimedia Laterna magika (Magic Lantern) company. In 1989, it became the underground nerve centre of the Velvet Revolution, where the Civic Forum thrashed out tactics in the dressing rooms and gave daily press conferences in the auditorium.

Church of Panna Maria Sněžná

Jungmannovo náměstí 18 ⓦ pms. ofm.cz. No set hours. Free. Once one of the great landmarks of Wenceslas Square, the church is now barely visible from any of the surrounding streets. To enter the church, go through the archway beside the Austrian Cultural Institute, behind the statue of Jungmann, and across the courtyard beyond. Founded in the fourteenth century by Emperor Charles IV, who envisaged a vast coronation church on a scale comparable with the St Vitus Cathedral, only the chancel got built before the money ran out. The result is curious – a church which is short in length, but equal to the cathedral in height. The 33 metre-high, prettily painted vaulting is awesome, as is the

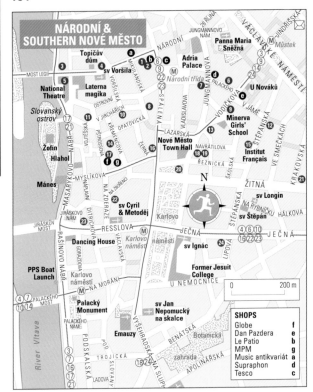

NÁRODNÍ & SOUTHERN NOVÉ MĚSTO

SHOPS	
Globe	f
Dan Pazdera	e
Le Patio	b
MPM	g
Music antikvariát	a
Supraphon	d
Tesco	c

EATING & DRINKING

Anis	7	Lemon Leaf	22	Posezení u Čiriny	19
Branický sklípek	9	Louvre	1	Potrefená husa	23
Break Café	12	Marathon	16	Shabu	6
Cicala	21	Novoměstský		Slavia	3
Dynamo	11	pivovar	13	U Fleků	14
Globe	17	Pivovarský dům	24	Velryba	8
Institut Français	15	Pizzeria Kmotra	10		

CLUBS & LIVE MUSIC

Divadlo Minor	18
MAT Studio	20
N11	4
National Theatre	5
Reduta	2

gold and black Baroque main altar which touches the ceiling.

Národní

It was on this busy street, lined with shops, galleries and clubs, that the Velvet Revolution began. On **November 17, 1989**, a 50,000-strong student demonstration worked its way down Národní aiming to reach Wenceslas Square. Halfway down the street their way was barred by the Communist riot-police. The students sat down and refused to disperse, some of them handing flowers out to the police. Suddenly, without any warning, the police attacked, and what became known as the *masakr* (massacre) began. In actual fact, no one was killed, though it wasn't for want of trying by the police. Under the arches of Národní 16, there's a small symbolic bronze relief of eight hands reaching out for help, a permanent shrine in memory of the hundreds who were hospitalized after the violence.

Further down Národní, on the right-hand side, is an eye-catching duo of Art Nouveau buildings. The first, at no. 7, was built for the **Prague Savings Bank**, hence the beautiful mosaic lettering above the windows advertizing *život* (life insurance) and *kapital* (loans), as well as help with your *důchod* (pension) and *věno* (dowry). Next door, the slightly more ostentatious **Topičův dům**, headquarters of the official state publishers, provides the perfect accompaniment, with a similarly ornate wrought-iron and glass canopy.

National Theatre

Národní 2 ✆ www.narodni-divadlo. cz. Overlooking the Vltava is the gold-crested National Theatre (Národní divadlo), proud symbol of the Czech nation. Refused money from the Habsburg state coffers, Czechs of all classes dug deep into their pockets to raise the funds. In June 1881, the theatre opened with a premiere of Smetana's *Libuše*. In August of the same year, fire ripped through the building, destroying everything except the outer walls. Within two years the whole thing was rebuilt and even the emperor contributed this time. The grand portal on the north side of the theatre is embellished with suitably triumphant allegorical figures, and, inside, every square centimetre is taken up with paintings and sculptures by leading artists of the Czech national revival.

Standing behind the old National Theatre, and in dramatic contrast with it, is the theatre's state-of-the-art extension, the opaque glass box of the Nová scéna, completed in 1983. It's one of those buildings most Praguers love to hate, though compared to much of Prague's Communist-era architecture, it's not that bad.

Café Slavia

Semtanovo nábřeží 2. Daily 9am–11pm. The *Café Slavia*, opposite the National Theatre, has been a favourite haunt of the city's writers, dissidents, artists and actors since the days of the First Republic. The Czech avant-garde movement, Devětsil, including Nobel Prize-winner Jaroslav Seifert, used to hold its meetings here in the 1920s. The café has been carelessly modernized since those arcadian days, but it still has a great riverside view and a copy of Manet's famous *Absinthe Drinker* canvas on the wall.

Střelecký ostrov

Most Legií. The Střelecký ostrov, or Shooters' Island, is where the army held their shooting practice, on and off, from the fifteenth until the nineteenth century. Closer to the other bank, and accessible via most Legií (Legion's Bridge), it became a favourite spot for a Sunday promenade, and is still popular, especially in summer. The first May Day demonstrations took place here in 1890.

Slovanský ostrov (Slav Island)

Masarykovo nábřeží. This island was formed as a result of the natural silting of the river in the eighteenth century. It's commonly known as **Žofín**, after the island's very yellow cultural centre, built in 1835 and named for Sophie, the mother of Emperor Franz-Josef I. Concerts, balls and other social gatherings take place here, and there's a

▲ UPPER FACADE OF U NOVÁKŮ, VODIČKOVA

good beer garden round the back; rowing boats can be hired in the summer.

At the southern tip of **Slovanský ostrov** stands the onion-domed Šítek water tower. Close by, spanning the narrow channel between the island and the river bank, is the striking, white functionalist box of the **Mánes** art gallery (Tues–Sun 10am–6pm). Designed in 1930, the gallery puts on consistently interesting contemporary exhibitions. There's also a café and an upstairs restaurant, suspended above the channel.

Vodičkova

Vodičkova is probably the most impressive of the streets which head south from Wenceslas Square. Of the handful of buildings worth checking out on the way, the most remarkable is **U Nováků** with its mosaic of bucolic frolicking and its delicate, ivy-like wrought-ironwork – look out for the frog-prince holding up a windowsill. Further down the street stands the imposing neo-Renaissance Minerva girls' school, covered in bright red sgraffito. Founded in 1866, it was the first such institution in Prague, and was notorious for the antics of its pupils, the "Minervans", who shocked bourgeois Czech society with their experimentation with fashion, drugs and sexual freedom.

Karlovo náměstí

Once Prague's biggest square, Karlovo náměstí's impressive proportions are no longer so easy to appreciate, obscured by trees and cut in two by a busy thoroughfare. It was created by Emperor Charles IV as Nové Město's cattle market and used by him for the grisly annual

▲ U NOVÁKŮ

public display of his impressive collection of saintly relics, though now it actually signals the southern limit of the city's main commercial district and the beginning of predominantly residential Nové Město.

Nové Město Town Hall

Karlovo náměstí 25. May–Sept daily 10am–6pm. 20Kč. Built in the fourteenth century, the Nové Město Town Hall (Novoměstská radnice) is one of the finest Gothic buildings in the city, sporting three impressive triangular gables embellished with intricate blind tracery. It was here that Prague's **first defenestration** took place on July 30, 1419, when the radical Hussite preacher Jan Želivský and his penniless religious followers stormed the building, mobbed the councillors and burghers, and threw twelve or thirteen of them (including the mayor) out of the town hall windows onto the pikes of the Hussite mob below, who clubbed any survivors to death. Václav IV, on hearing the news, suffered a stroke and died just two weeks later. So began the long and bloody Hussite Wars. After the amalgamation of Prague's separate towns in 1784, the building was used solely as a criminal court and prison. Nowadays, you can visit the site of the defenestration, and climb to the top of the tower (added shortly afterwards) for a view over central Prague. The town hall also puts on temporary art exhibitions.

Church of sv Ignác

Karlovo náměstí. No set hours. Free. Begun in 1665, this former Jesuit church is quite remarkable inside, a pink and white confection, with lots of frothy stucco work and an exuberant pulpit dripping with gold drapery, cherubs and saints. The statue of St Ignatius, which sits above the entrance surrounded by a sunburst, caused controversy at the time, as until then only the Holy Trinity had been depicted in such a way.

▲ NOVÉ MĚSTO TOWN HALL

Cathedral of sv Cyril and Metoděj (Heydrich Martyrs' Monument)

Resslova 9 ☎ 224 920 686. Tues–Sun: April–Oct 10am–5pm; Nov–March 10am–4pm. 50Kč. Amid all the traffic, it's extremely difficult to imagine the scene at this church on June 18, 1942, when seven Czechoslovak secret agents were besieged in the church

PLACES

Národní and southern Nové Město

by hundreds of Waffen SS. The agents had pulled off the dramatic assassination of Nazi leader **Reinhard Heydrich**, but had been betrayed by one of their own men. The Nazis surrounded the church just after 4am and fought a pitched battle for over six hours, trying explosives, flooding and any other method they could think of to drive the men out of their stronghold in the crypt. Eventually, all seven agents committed suicide rather than give themselves up. There's a plaque at street level on the south wall commemorating those who died, and an exhibition and video on the whole affair situated in the crypt itself, which has been left pretty much as it was; the entrance is underneath the church steps on Na Zderaze.

Dancing House

Rašínovo nábřeží 80. Designed by the Canadian-born Frank O. Gehry and the Yugoslav-born Vlado Milunič, this building is known as the Dancing House (Tančící dům) or "Fred and Ginger", after the shape of the building's two towers, which look vaguely like a couple ballroom dancing. The apartment block next door was built at the turn of the twentieth century by Havel's grandfather, and was where, until the early 1990s, Havel and his first wife, Olga, lived in the top-floor flat.

Palacký Monument

Palackého náměstí. After the Hus Monument, this Monument to František Palacký, the great nineteenth-century Czech historian, politician and nationalist, is probably Prague's finest Art Nouveau sculpture. Fifteen years in the making, it was finally completed in 1912 and found universal disfavour.

The critics have mellowed over the years, and nowadays it's appreciated for what it is – an energetic and inspirational piece of work. Ethereal bronze bodies, representing the world of the imagination, shoot out at all angles, contrasting sharply with the plain stone mass of the plinth, and below, the giant seated figure of Palacký himself, representing the real world.

▲ PALACKÝ MONUMENT

Emauzy monastery

Vyšehradská 49. Mon–Fri 9am–4pm. 30Kč. The intertwined concrete spires of the Emauzy monastery are an unusual modern addition to the Prague skyline. The monastery was one of the few important historical buildings to be damaged in the last war, in this case by a stray Anglo-American bomb (the pilot thought he was over Dresden). Founded by Emperor Charles IV, the cloisters contain some extremely valuable Gothic frescoes.

Shops

Globe
Pštrossova 6 ⓦ www.globebookstore.
cz. Daily 10am–midnight. The expat
bookstore *par excellence* – both a
social centre and superbly well-
stocked store, with an adjacent
café and friendly staff.

Jan Pazdera
Vodičkova 28. Mon–Fri 10am–6pm.
Truly spectacular selection of old
and new cameras, microscopes,
telescopes, opera glasses and
binoculars.

Le Patio
Národní 22. Mon–Sat 10am–7pm,
Sun 11am–7pm. Café selling arty
wrought-ironwork from chairs
and chandeliers to bottle-racks
and birdcages.

MPM
Myslíkova 19 ⓦ www.mpm.cz. Mon–Fri
10am–6pm. Kits for making model
planes, tanks, trains, ships and
cars, and toy soldiers.

Music antikvariát
Národní 25. Mon–Sat 10.30am–7pm.
The best secondhand record store
in Prague, particularly good for
jazz and folk, but also rock/pop
– though there's not much in the
way of classical.

Supraphon
Jungmannova 20. Mon–Fri 9am–7pm,
Sat 9am–1pm. This former state
record company shop stocks
all sorts of music, but excels in
classical.

Tesco
Národní 26. Mon–Fri 8am–9pm, Sat
9am–8pm, Sun 10am–8pm. Neo-
functionalist store on four floors,
selling a good mix of Czech and
imported goods. Bears absolutely
no resemblance to its British

supermarket namesake, beyond
its neon sign.

Cafés

Anis
Jungmannova 21. Mon–Fri 10.30am–
7pm, Sat 11am–5pm. Arabic fast
food – stuffed vine leaves, felafal,
taboule and a salad bar – with
either self-service sit-in or
takeaway, a stone's throw from
Wenceslas Square.

Break Café
Štěpánská 32. Mon–Fri 8am–10pm,
Sat 9.30am–7pm. Stylish, modern
café, popular with expats. There
are muffins, toast and croissants
for breakfast; salads, burgers
and grilled panini for lunch; and
everything from *bramborák* to
lasagne and oysters for dinner.

Globe
Pštrossova 6 ⓦ www.globebookstore.
cz. Daily 10am–midnight. Large,
buzzing café, at the back of the
English-language bookstore of
the same name that's a popular
expat hang-out, but enjoyable
nevertheless, with live music on
Friday and Saturday evenings.

Institut Français
Štěpánská 35 ⓦ www.ifp.cz. Mon & Fri
8.30am–7pm, Tues–Thurs 8.30am–
7.30pm, Sat 10am–3pm. Housed in
the French cultural centre, the
Institut's great coffee and superb
French pastries – plus of course
the chance to pose with a French
newspaper – make this one of
Prague's best-loved cafés.

Louvre
Národní 20 ⓦ www.kavarny.cz/louvre.
Daily 8am–11pm. Turn-of-the-
century café, closed down under
the Communists but now back
in business and a very popular

▲ MARATHON CAFÉ

refuelling spot for Prague's shoppers. Dodgy colour scheme, but high ceiling, mirrors, daily papers, lots of cakes, a billiard hall and window seats overlooking Národní.

Marathon

Černá 9. Mon–Fri 10am–10pm.
Smoky, self-styled "library café" in the university's 1920s-style religious faculty, hidden in the backstreets, south of Národní.

Shabu

Palackého 11. Daily 10am–midnight.
Tiny little café down a passageway, serving an interesting selection of Yugoslav snacks such as grilled aubergine, Balkan salad and *burek*.

Slavia

Semtanovo nábřeží 2. Daily 9am–11pm.
Famous 1920s riverside café still pulls in a mixed crowd from shoppers and tourists to older folk and the pre- and post-theatre mob.

Velryba (The Whale)

Opatovická 24. Daily 11am–2am. One of the most determinedly cool student cafés in Prague – smoky, loud and serving cheap Czech food (plus several veggie options) and a wide range of malt whiskies.

Restaurants

Cicala

Žitná 43 ☎ 222 210 375, ⓦ trattoria. cicala.cz. Mon–Sat 11.30am–10.30pm.
Very good little Italian basement restaurant specializing (mid-week) in fresh seafood (from 300Kč). There's also a wide range of pasta (220Kč) and an appetizing antipasto selection.

Dynamo

Pštrossova 29 ☎ 224 932 020.
Daily 11.30am–midnight. Trendy little spot with eye-catching retro-1960s designer decor, an incredible single malt whisky selection and competent fish, chicken, steak and pasta dishes for 250Kč upwards.

Lemon Leaf

Myslíkova 14 ☎ 224 919 056, ⓦ www.lemon.cz. Mon–Thurs 11am–11pm, Fri 11am–12.30am, Sat 12.30pm–12.30am, Sun 12.30pm–11pm. Attractive, popular Thai restaurant, with spicy meat and fish curries for around 200Kč.

Pizzeria Kmotra (Godmother)

V jirchářích 12 ☎ 224 915 809, ⓦ www.kmotra.cz. Daily 11am–midnight. This inexpensive, sweaty, basement pizza place is one of Prague's most popular, and justifiably so – if possible, book a table in advance. Pizzas 100–150Kč.

Posezení u Čiriny

Navrátilova 6 ☎ 222 231 709. Mon–Sat 11am–11pm. A little family-run place, with only a handful of tables inside, leather benches in pleasant wooden alcoves, and a summer terrace. Classic Slovak home cooking for around 200Kč.

Pubs

Branický sklípek

Vodičkova 26. Mon–Fri 9am–11pm, Sat & Sun 11am–11pm. Convenient downtown pub (aka *U Purkmistra*) decked out like a pine furniture showroom serving typical Czech fare and jugs of Prague's Braník beer. The rough-and-ready *Branická formanka* next door opens and closes earlier.

Novoměstský pivovar

Vodičkova 20 ⓦ www.npivovar. cz. Mon–Fri 10am–11.30pm, Sat 11.30am–11.30pm, Sun noon–10pm. Micro-brewery which serves its own misty home brew, plus Czech food, in a series of bright, sprawling modern beer halls.

Pivovarský dům

Corner of Lipová/Ječná. Daily 11am–11.30pm. Busy micro-brewery dominated by big, shiny copper vats, serving light, mixed and dark unfiltered beer (plus banana, coffee and wheat varieties), and all the standard Czech pub dishes (including *pivný sýr*).

Potrefená husa (The Wounded Goose)

Jiráskovo náměstí 1. Daily 11.30am–1am. Smart, convivial brick cellar pub that attracts a mix of young and middle-aged professionals, with Staropramen and decent pub food.

U Fleků

Křemencova 11. Daily 9am–11pm. Famous medieval *pivnice* where the unique dark 13° beer, Flek, has been exclusively brewed and consumed since 1499. Seats over 500 German tourists at a go, serves short measures (0.4l), slaps an extra charge on for the music and still you might have to queue to get in. This is a real tourist trap, and the only reason to visit is to sample the beer, which you're best off doing during the day.

▲ U FLEKŮ

Clubs and the performing arts

Divadlo minor

Vodičkova 6 ☎ 222 231 351, ⓦ www. minor.cz. The former state puppet theatre puts on children's shows most days, plus adult shows on occasional evenings, sometimes with English subtitles.

PLACES Národní and southern Nové Město

Laterna magika
(Magic Lantern)

Nová scéna, Národní 4 ☎ 224 931 482, ⓦ www.laterna.cz. The National Theatre's Nová scéna, one of Prague's most modern and versatile stages, is the main base for Laterna magika, founders of multimedia and "black light" theatre way back in 1958. Their slick productions continue effortlessly to pull in crowds of tourists.

MAT Studio

Karlovo náměstí 19 ☎ 224 915 765, ⓦ www.mat.cz. Tiny café and cinema popular with the film crowd, with an eclectic programme of shorts, documentaries and Czech films with English subtitles. The entrance is on Odborů.

N11

Národní 11 ☎ 222 075 705, ⓦ www. n11.cz. Tues–Sun. Funky, medium-sized, central club with several bars, an OK restaurant, a decent sound system and DJs who play a whole range of dance tunes from hip-hop to Latin, plus the occasional live act.

National Theatre
(Národní divadlo)

Národní 2 ☎ 224 901 487, ⓦ www. narodni-divadlo.cz. Prague's grandest nineteenth-century theatre is the living embodiment of the Czech national revival movement, and continues to put on a wide variety of mostly, though by no means exclusively, Czech plays, plus the odd opera and ballet. Worth visiting for the decor alone.

Reduta

Národní 20 ☎ 224 912 246, ⓦ ww. redutajazzclub.cz. Prague's best-known jazz club – Bill Clinton played his sax here in front of Havel – attracts a very touristy crowd, but also some decent acts. Gigs daily from 9.30pm.

Vyšehrad, Vinohrady and Žižkov

The fortress of Vyšehrad makes for a perfect afternoon escape away from the human congestion of the city centre: its cemetery shelters the remains of Bohemia's artistic elite; the ramparts afford superb views over the river; and below the fortress there are several interesting examples of Czech Cubist architecture. Vinohrady, to the east, is a late nineteenth-century residential suburb, dominated by long streets of grandiose apartment blocks, with one or two specific sights to guide your wandering. By contrast, Žižkov, further north, is a grittier working-class district, whose shabby, slightly seedy streets contain some of the city's best pubs and clubs.

Vyšehrad

V pevnosti 5b Ⓦ www.praha-vysehrad. cz. Open 24hr. Free. The rocky red-brick fortress of Vyšehrad – literally "High Castle" – has more myths attached to it than any other place in Bohemia. According to Czech legend, this is the place where the Slav tribes first settled in Prague and where the "wise and tireless chieftain" Krok built a castle, whence his youngest daughter Libuše went on to found Praha itself. Alas, the archeological evidence doesn't really bear this claim out. What you see now are the remains of a fortified barracks built by the Habsburgs and then turned into a public park.

You can explore the fortress **dungeons**, or *kasematy* (daily: April–Oct 9.30am–6pm; Nov–March 9.30am–5pm; 30Kč), which you enter via the northern entrance, or Cihelná brána. After a short guided tour of a section of the underground passageways underneath the ramparts, you enter a vast storage hall, which shelters several of the original statues from the Charles Bridge, and, when the lights are switched off, reveals a camera obscura image of a tree.

Church of sv Petr and Pavel

K rotundě 10. Sat & Sun 10am–noon & 1–4pm. Free. The fortress's chief landmark is this blackened sandstone church, rebuilt in the 1880s in neo-Gothic style on the site of an eleventh-century

Getting to Vyšehrad

To reach Vyšehrad, take tram #3, #7, #16, #17 or #21 to Výtoň, and either wind your way up Vratislavova to the Cihelná brána or take the steep stairway from Rašínovo nábřeží that leads up through the trees. Alternatively, from Vyšehrad metro station, walk west past the ugly Prague Congress Centre, and enter via V pevnosti, where there's an information centre (daily: April–Oct 9.30am–6pm; Nov–March 9.30am–5pm).

PLACES

Vyšehrad, Vinohrady and Žižkov

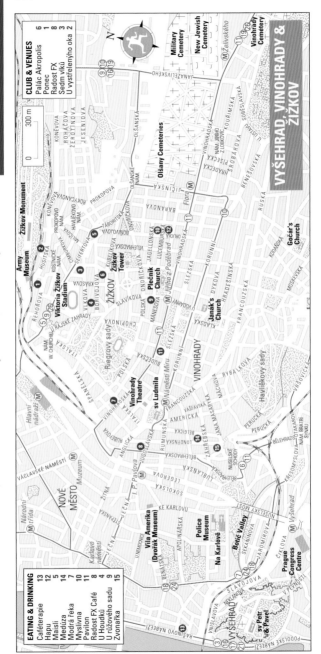

▲ CHURCH OF SV PETR AND PAVEL

PLACES

basilica. The twin open-work spires are now the fortress's most familiar landmark, and if luck is on your side, you'll be able to have a look at the church's polychrome interior, though opening times can be a bit erratic.

Vyšehrad Cemetery (Vyšehradský hřbitov)

Daily: March, April & Oct 8am–6pm; May–Sept 8am–7pm; Nov–Feb 8am–5pm. Free. Most Czechs come to Vyšehrad to pay a visit to the cemetery. It's a measure of the part that artists and intellectuals played in the foundation of the nation, and the regard in which they are still held, that the most prestigious graveyard in the city is given over to them: no soldiers, no politicians – not even the Communists managed to muscle their way in here (except on artistic merit). Sheltered from the wind by its high walls, lined on two sides by delicate arcades, it's a tiny cemetery (reflecting, as it were, the size of the nation) filled with well-kept graves, many of them designed by the country's leading sculptors.

To the uninitiated only a handful of figures are well known, but for the Czechs the place is alive with great names (there's a useful plan of the most notable graves at the entrance nearest the church). Ladislav Šaloun's grave for **Dvořák**, situated under the arches, is one of the more showy ones, with a mosaic inscription, studded with gold stones, glistening behind wrought-iron railings. **Smetana**, who died twenty years earlier, is buried in comparatively modest surroundings near the Slavín Monument, the cemetery's focal point, which is the communal resting place of more than fifty Czech artists, including the painter Alfons Mucha and the opera singer Ema Destinová.

The grave of the Romantic poet Karel Hynek Mácha was the assembly point for the demonstration on November 17, 1989 which triggered the Velvet Revolution.

▲ VYŠEHRAD CEMETERY

Cubist villas

Even if you harbour only a passing interest in modern architecture, it's worth seeking out the cluster of Cubist villas below the fortress in Vyšehrad. The most impressive example is the apartment block at Neklanova 30, begun in 1913, which brilliantly exploits its angular location. Further along Neklanova at no. 2, there's another Cubist facade, and around the corner is the most ambitious of the lot, the Kovařovicova vila, which uses prism shapes and angular lines to produce the sharp geometric contrasts of light and dark shadows characteristic of Cubist painting.

Prague Congress Centre

5 května 65 @ www.kcp.cz. The Prague Congress Centre (Kongresové centrum) is a low-lying, supremely ugly concrete carbuncle, formerly known as the Palác kultury and originally used for Communist Party congresses. It remains the country's biggest concert venue, but the best thing about it is the view north over the Nuselský most, which spans the Botič valley, to Na Karlově church (see below).

Police Museum

Ke Karlovu 1 @ www.mvcr.cz. Tues–Sun 10am–5pm. 20Kč. The former Augustinian monastery of Karlov houses the Muzeum Policie, which concentrates on road and traffic offences, and the force's latest challenges: forgery, drugs and murder. It's mildly diverting, with several participatory displays, including a quiz on the Highway Code (in Czech), a mini road layout for kids' trikes and bikes, and a particularly gruesome section on forensic science.

Na Karlově church

Ke Karlovu. No set hours. Free. Founded by Emperor Charles IV and designed in imitation of Charlemagne's tomb in Aachen, this monastic church is quite unlike any other in Prague. If it's open, you should take a look at the dark interior, which was remodelled in the sixteenth century by Bonifaz Wohlmut. The stellar vault has no central supporting pillars – a remarkable feat of engineering for its time, and one which gave rise to numerous legends about the architect being in league with the devil.

Vila Amerika (Dvořák Museum)

Ke Karlovu 20. Tues–Sun: April–Sept 10am–1.30pm & 2–5.30pm; Oct–March 9.30am–1.30pm & 2–5pm. 50Kč. The russet-coloured Vila Amerika was originally named after the local pub, but is now a museum devoted to Czech composer Antonín Dvořák (1841–1904), the most famous of all Czech composers, who lived for a time on nearby Zitná. Even if you've no interest in Dvořák, the house itself is a delight, built as a Baroque summer palace around 1720. The tasteful period rooms, with the composer's music wafting in and out, and the tiny garden dotted with Baroque sculptures, compensate for what the display cabinets may lack.

Náměstí Míru

If Vinohrady has a centre, it's the leafy square of náměstí Míru, a good introduction to the aspirations of this confident, bourgeois neighbourhood. At its centre stands the brick-built basilica of sv Ludmila, designed in the late 1880s in a severe neo-Gothic style, though the interior furnishings have the odd flourish of Art Nouveau. In front of the church is a statue commemorating the Čapek brothers, writer Karel and painter Josef, who together symbolized the golden era of the interwar republic. Karel died in 1938, shortly after the Nazi invasion, while Josef perished in Belsen seven years later; their influence was deliberately underplayed by the Communists, and the memorial was erected only in the 1990s. Two more buildings on the square deserve attention, the most flamboyant being the **Vinohrady Theatre** (Divadlo na Vinohradech), built in 1907, using Art Nouveau and neo-Baroque elements in equal measure. More subdued, but equally ornate inside and out, is the district's former Národní dům, a grandiose neo-Renaissance edifice from the 1890s housing a ballroom/concert hall and restaurant.

for detail; look out for the little gold crosses inset into the brickwork like stars, inside and out, and the celestial orbs of light suspended above the heads of the congregation.

Žižkov Tower (Televizní vysílač)

Mahlerovy sady 1 ⓦ www.tower.cz. Daily 10am–11pm. 150Kč. At 216m in height, the Žižkov TV tower is the tallest building in Prague. Close up, it's an intimidating futuristic piece of architecture, made all the more disturbing by the addition of several statues of giant babies crawling up the sides, courtesy of artist David Černý. Begun in the 1970s in a desperate bid to jam West German television transmissions, the tower became fully operational only in the 1990s. In the course of its construction, however, the Communists saw fit to demolish part of a nearby Jewish cemetery

Plečnik church

Náměstí Jiřího z Poděbrad. No set hours. Free. Prague's most celebrated modern church is **Nejsvětějšího Srdce Páně** (Most Sacred Heart of Our Lord), built in 1928 by the Slovene architect Josip Plečnik. It's a marvellously eclectic and individualistic work, employing a sophisticated potpourri of architectural styles: a Neoclassical pediment and a great slab of a clock tower with a giant transparent face in imitation of a Gothic rose window, as well as the bricks and mortar of contemporary constructivism. Plečnik also had a sharp eye

▲ PLEČNIK CHURCH

that had served the community between 1787 and 1891; a small section survives to the northwest of the tower. From the fifth-floor café or the viewing platform on the eighth floor, you can enjoy a spectacular view across Prague.

PLACES

Vyšehrad, Vinohrady and Žižkov

▲ ŽIŽKOV TOWER

Olšany cemeteries (Olšany hřbitovy)

Vinohradská. Daily dawn–dusk. Free.
The vast Olšany cemeteries were originally created for the victims of the great plague epidemic of 1680. The perimeter walls are lined with glass cabinets, stacked like shoe-boxes, containing funereal urns and mementoes, while the graves themselves are a mixed bag of artistic achievements, reflecting the funereal fashions of the day as much as the character of the deceased. The cemeteries are divided into districts and crisscrossed with cobbled streets; at each gate there's a map and an aged janitor ready to point you in the right direction.

The cemeteries' two most famous incumbents are an ill-fitting couple: **Klement Gottwald**, the country's first Communist president, whose remains were removed from the mausoleum on Žižkov hill after 1989 and reinterred here; and **Jan Palach**, the philosophy student who set light to himself in January 1969 in protest at the Soviet occupation. More than 750,000 people attended Palach's funeral in January 1969, and in an attempt to put a stop to the annual vigils at his graveside, the secret police removed his body and reburied him in his home town outside Prague. In 1990, Palach's body was returned to Olšany; you'll find it just to the east of the main entrance.

New Jewish Cemetery (Nový židovský hřbitov)

Fibichova. April–Sept Mon–Thurs & Sun 9am–4.30pm, Fri 9am–2.30pm; Oct–March Mon–Thurs & Sun 9am–3.30pm, Fri 9am–1.30pm. Free.
Founded in the 1890s, the New Jewish Cemetery was designed to last for a century, with room for 100,000 graves. It's a melancholy spot, particularly so in the east of the cemetery, where large empty allotments wait in vain to be filled by the generation that perished in the Holocaust. Most people come here to visit **Franz Kafka's grave**, 400m east along the south wall and signposted from the entrance. He is buried, along with his mother and father (both of whom outlived him), beneath a plain headstone; the plaque below commemorates his three sisters who died in the camps.

Žižkov Hill

Žižkov Hill is the thin green wedge of land that separates Žižkov from Karlín, the grid-plan industrial district to the north. From its westernmost point, which juts out almost to the edge of Nové Město, is the definitive panoramic view over the city centre. It was here, on July 14, 1420, that the Hussites enjoyed their first and finest victory at the **Battle of Vítkov**, under the inspired leadership of the one-eyed general, Jan Žižka (hence the name of the district). Ludicrously outnumbered by more than ten to one, Žižka and his fanatically motivated troops thoroughly trounced the Bohemian King and Holy Roman Emperor Sigismund and his papal forces.

Despite its totalitarian aesthetics, the giant concrete **Žižkov monument** (Ⓦ www.pamatnik-vitkov.cz), which graces the crest of the hill, was actually built between the wars as a memorial to the Czechoslovak Legion who fought against the Habsburgs in the World War I – the gargantuan statue of the mace-wielding Žižka, which fronts the monument, is reputedly the world's largest equestrian statue. The building was later used by the Nazis as an arsenal, and eventually became a Communist mausoleum. In 1990, the Communists were cremated and quietly reinterred in Olšany. The monument is currently being renovated, a museum is being installed inside and a café on top, with a tentative completion date of 2009.

Army Museum (Armádní muzeum)

U památníku 2 Ⓦ www.militarymuseum.cz. Tues–Sun 10am–6pm. Free. Guarded by a handful of unmanned tanks, howitzers and armoured vehicles, the Army Museum has a permanent exhibition covering the country's military history from 1914 to 1945. A fairly evenly balanced

▲ ARMY MUSEUM

account of both world wars includes coverage of controversial subjects such as the exploits of the Czechoslovak Legion, the Heydrich assassination and the 1945 Prague Uprising.

Cafés

Caféterapie

Na Hrobci 3. Mon–Fri 10am–10pm, Sat & Sun noon–10pm. Small, simply furnished café that serves up nice healthy Med-influenced salads, sandwiches, toasties and a few hot dishes.

Medúza

Belgická 17. Mon–Fri 10am–1am, Sat & Sun noon–1am. A trendy young crowd hangs out in this deliberately faded, inexpensive café, which serves breakfast all day and gets packed out most evenings.

Pavilon

Vinohradská 50 Ⓦ www.ambi.cz. Mon–Fri 8am–10pm, Sat & Sun 9am–10pm. Wonderful café serving great breakfasts and fresh pasta for lunch, situated in the heart of Vinohrady's regenerated covered market.

Radost FX Café

Bělehradská 120 Ⓦ www.radostfx.cz. Daily 11.30am–4am. Good choice of vegetarian dishes, all for under 200Kč, plus funky music. Popular with the expat posse, particularly

PLACES

Vyšehrad, Vinohrady and Žižkov

for the Sunday brunch.

Restaurants

Mailsi
Lipanská 1 ☎ 222 717 783. Daily 11am–1am. Prague's only Pakistani restaurant is a friendly, unpretentious place that's great for a comfort curry for around 300Kč, as hot as you can handle.

Modrá řeka (Blue River)
Mánesova 13 ☎ 222 251 601. Mon–Fri 11am–11pm, Sat & Sun 5–11pm. Family-run Bosnian Muslim restaurant with attentive service, and good Balkan home cooking.

Myslivna (The Hunting Lodge)
Jagellonskáa 21 ☎ 222 723 252. Daily 11.30am–4.30pm & 6–11.30pm. A hearty game restaurant in the suburbs, serving up excellent venison and quail, all for under 300Kč.

Pubs and bars

Hapu
Orlická 8. Mon–Sat 6pm–2am. Chilled-out Žižkov cocktail bar without the snooty/uptight factor but with lots of great mixes and comfy sofas.

U Houdků
Bořivojova 110. Daily 10am–11pm. Friendly local pub in the heart of Žižkov with a beer garden, Velkopopvický kozel and cheap Czech food.

U růžového sadu (The Rose Garden)
Mánesova 89. Mon–Thurs 10.30am–midnight, Fri & Sat 10.30am–1am, Sun 11.30am–10pm. Imaginatively decorated for a Czech pub and perfectly situated if you're visiting Plečnik's Church.

Zvonařka (The Bell)
Šafaříkova 1. Daily 11am–midnight. The slick, futuristic bar has a terrace with great views over the Nuselské schody and Botič valley.

Clubs and live music

Palác Akropolis
Kubelíkova 27 🌐 www.akropolis.cz. Café/bar daily 7pm–5am. Prague's very popular smoke-filled world music venue is also a great place to just have a drink or a bite to eat, as well as checking out the live gigs.

Ponec
Husitská 24a 🌐 www.divadloponec. cz. Former cinema, now an innovative dance venue and centre for the annual Tanec Praha dance festival in June/July.

Radost FX
Bělehradská 120 ☎ 224 254 776, 🌐 www.radostfx.cz. Thurs–Sat 10pm–4am. The longest-running all-round dance club venue in Prague, attracting the usual mix of clubbers and expats.

Sedm vlků (Seven Wolves)
Vlkova 33. Mon–Sat 5pm–3am. Club-bar with a penchant for reggae and resident DJs who make the most of the impressive sound system.

U vystřelenýho oka (The Shot-Out Eye)
U božích bojovníků 3. Mon–Sat 4.30pm–1am. Big, loud, smoky, heavy-drinking pub with unusually good (occasionally live) indie rock and lashings of Měšťan beer, plus absinthe chasers.

Holešovice

Tucked into a huge U-bend in the River Vltava, the late nineteenth-century suburb of Holešovice boasts two huge splodges of green: Letná, overlooking the city centre, and, to the north, Stromovka, the city's largest public park, bordering the Výstaviště funfair and trade fair grounds. A stroll through the park gives you access to the Baroque chateau of Troja and the city's leafy zoo. However, the single most important sight in Holešovice is the Veletržní Palace, which houses the city's main Museum of Modern Art. Only a trickle of tourists makes it out here, but it's worth the effort, if only to remind yourself that Prague doesn't begin and end at the Charles Bridge.

Veletržní Palace (Trade Fair Palace)

Dukelských hrdinů 45 ⓦwww. ngprague.cz. Tues–Sun 10am–6pm. 160Kč. The Veletržní Palace gets nothing like the number of visitors it should. For not only does the building house the city's best nineteenth- and twentieth-century Czech and international art collection, it is also an architectural sight in itself. Built in 1928, the palace is Prague's ultimate functionalist masterpiece, not so much from the outside, but inside, where its gleaming white vastness is suitably awesome.

The gallery is both big and bewildering, and virtually impossible to view in its entirety in a single visit. Special exhibitions occupy the ground, first and fifth floors, while the permanent collection occupies the second, third and fourth floors. The popular French art collection can be found on the third floor, and includes works by Rodin, Renoir, Van Gogh, Matisse and Picasso. Also on this floor, you'll find works by the Czech Cubists Čapek,

Gutfreund, Filla and Kubišta, and a whole series of works by František Kupka, by far the most important Czech painter of the last century, who secured his place in the history of art by being (possibly) the first artist in the western world to exhibit abstract paintings. The rest of the "foreign art" is on the first floor, where you'll get to see, among other things, a Surrealist Miró, a couple of Henry Moore sculptures and a perforated Lucio Fontana canvas, plus a few canvases by Klimt, Kokoschka, Schiele and Munch, whose influence on early twentieth-century Czech art was considerable.

In the nineteenth-century collection, on the fourth floor, you'll find an exhaustive overview of Czech art of the period, while the second floor collection takes you from 1930 to the present day – it, too, is mostly Czech in origin, and gives a pretty good introduction to the country's artistic peaks and troughs. Fans of Communist kitsch should make their way to the excellent Socialist

EATING & DRINKING

Le Bistrot De Marlène	3
La Crêperie	8
Delicatesse	7
Fraktal	6
Hanavský pavilón	10
Letenské zameček	9
Orange	4
Svatá Klara	1
U houbaře	5

CLUBS & LIVE MUSIC

Mecca	2

HOLEŠOVICE

N

LIBEŇ

Botanic Gardens

Troja Castle

TROJA

Zoo

Císařský ostrov

River Vltava

Stromovka

VÝSTAVIŠTĚ

Praha-Holešovice
Nádraží Holešovice

Divadlo Spirála

Maroldovo panorama
Průmysl Palace
Planetárium

Křižíkova fontána

Lapidárium

Mořský Svět

Pivní galerie

HOLEŠOVICE

Veletržní Palace

National Technical Museum

Sparta stadiums

LETNÁ

Metronome

Bilkova vila

BUBENEČ

TROJSKÁ

POVLTAVSKÁ

V HOLEŠOVIČKÁCH

MOST BARIKÁDNÍKŮ

U VLTAVY

JANCOVKOVA

V HÁJI

NA MANINÁCH

U PRŮHONU

OSADNI

DĚLNICKÁ

TUSAROVA

JATEČNÍ

ARGENTINSKÁ

PLYNÁRNÍ

ŽELEZNIČÁŘŮ

BUBENSKÁ

VELETRŽNÍ

ŠMALVÍ

HERMANOVA

SOCHORA

STRESSMAYEROVA NÁM.

DUKELSKÝCH HRDINŮ

KOSTELNÍ

VEVERKOVA

HORÁKOVO

KAMENICKÁ

MILADY HORÁKOVÉ

LETOHRADSKÁ

DOBROVSKÉHO

OVENECKÁ

ČECHOVA

ESMERALOVA

NAD KRÁLOV

NÁM. POD KAŠTANY

KRUPKOVO NÁM.

PELLÉOVA

BUBENEČSKÁ

EISNEROVA

PLEŠNOVO NÁM.

SIBELIUS NÁM.

VERDUNSKÁ

TERRONSKÁ

VE STRUHÁCH

ČS. ARMÁDY

DEJVICKÁ

HRADČANSKÁ

Chotkovy sady

JUGOSLÁVSKÝCH PARTYZÁNŮ

SVATOVÍTSKÁ

LIBEŇSKÝ MOST

River Vltava

Ostrov Štvanice

HLÁVKŮV MOST

ŠTEFÁNIKŮV MOST

NÁBŘ. KPT. JAROŠE

NÁBŘ. E. BENEŠE

ROHANSKÉ NÁBŘ.

0   400 m

Realism section, heralded by Karel Pokorný's monumental *Fraternisation* sculpture, in which a Czechoslovak soldier is engaging in a "kiss of death" with a Soviet comrade. Performance art (umění akce) was big in the 1960s, even in Communist Czechoslovakia, and it, too, has its own section, which is undoubtedly worth a giggle. The gallery also owns several works by Jiří Kolář – pronounced "collage" – who, coincidentally, specializes in collages of random words and reproductions of other people's paintings.

National Technical Museum (Národní technické muzeum)

Kostelní 42 ☏ 220 399 111, ⊛ www. ntm.cz. Closed for renovation.

Despite its dull title, this museum is surprisingly interesting, with a showpiece hangar-like main hall containing an impressive gallery of motorbikes, Czech and foreign, and a wonderful collection of old planes, trains and automobiles from Czechoslovakia's industrial heyday between the wars when the country's Škoda cars and Tatra soft-top stretch limos were really something to brag about.

The oldest car in the collection is Laurin & Klement's 1898 Präsident, more of a motorized carriage than a car; the museum also boasts the oldest Bugatti in the world. Other displays trace the development of early photography, and there's also a collection of some of Kepler and Tycho Brahe's astrological instruments. The museum is due to reopen in summer 2008, though don't count on it.

Letná

A high plateau hovering above the city, the flat green expanse of the Letná plain has long been the traditional assembly point for invading and besieging armies. Under the Communists, it was used primarily for the annual May Day parades, during which thousands trudged past the Sparta Prague stadium, where the Communist leaders would salute from their giant red podium. It once boasted the largest **Stalin monument** in the world: a thirty-metre-high granite sculpture portraying a procession of Czechs and Russians being led to Communism by the Pied Piper figure of Stalin, but popularly dubbed *tlačenice* (the

▲ NATIONAL TECHNICAL MUSEUM

PLACES Holešovice

crush) because of its resemblance to a Communist-era bread queue. The monument was unveiled on May 1, 1955, but within a year Khrushchev had denounced Stalin, and the monument was blown up in 1962. On the site of the Stalin statue, overlooking the Vltava, stands David Černý's symbolic giant red **metronome** (which is lit up at night).

▲ BÍLKOVA VILA

Bílkova vila

Mieckiewiczova 1. Sat & Sun 10am–5pm. 50Kč. The Bílkova vila honours one of the most original of all Czech sculptors, František Bílek (1872–1941). Built in 1911 to the artist's own design, the house was intended as both a "cathedral of art" and the family home. Inside, Bílek's extravagant religious sculptures line the walls of his "workshop and temple". In addition to his sculptural and relief work in wood and stone, often wildly expressive and spiritually tortured, there are also ceramics, graphics and a few mementoes of Bílek's life. His living quarters have also been restored and have much of the original wooden furniture, designed and carved by Bílek himself, still in place. Check out the dressing table for his wife, shaped like some giant church lectern, and the wardrobe

decorated with a border of hearts, a penis, a nose, an ear and an eye plus the sun, stars and moon.

Chotkovy sady

Prague's first public park, the Chotkovy sady, was founded in 1833 by the ecologically minded city governor, Count Chotek. The atmosphere here is relaxed and you can happily stretch out on the grass and soak up the sun, or head for the south wall, for an unrivalled view of the bridges and islands of the Vltava. At the centre of the park there's a bizarre, melodramatic grotto-like memorial to the nineteenth-century Romantic poet **Julius Zeyer**, an elaborate monument from which life-sized characters from Zeyer's works, carved in white marble, emerge from the blackened rocks.

▲ CHOTKOVY SADY

Výstaviště (Exhibition Grounds)

Dukelských hrdinů. Tues–Fri 2–10pm, Sat & Sun 10am–10pm. Free.
Since the 1891 Prague Exhibition, Výstaviště has served as the city's main trade fair arena and funfair. At the centre of the complex is the flamboyant stained-glass and wrought-iron Průmysl Palace, scene of Communist Party rubber-stamp congresses. Several modern structures were built for the 1991 Prague Exhibition, including a circular theatre, Divadlo Spirála.

The grounds are busiest at the weekend, particularly in summer, when hordes of Prague families descend on the place to wolf down hot dogs and drink beer. Apart from the annual trade fairs and special exhibitions, there are a few permanent attractions: the city's **Planetárium** (Mon–Thurs 8.30am–noon & 1–8pm, Sat & Sun 9.30am–noon & 1–8pm; 20Kč; Ⓦwww.planetarium.cz), which has static displays and shows videos; the **Maroldovo**

▲ PRŮMYSL PALACE

panorama (Tues–Fri 2–5pm, Sat & Sun 11am–5pm; 20Kč), a giant diorama of the 1434 Battle of Lipany; and **Mořský svět** (daily 10am–7pm; 240Kč; Ⓦwww.morsky-svet.cz), an aquarium full of countless colourful tropical fish, a few rays and some sea turtles. In the long summer evenings, there's also an open-air cinema (*letní kino*), and hourly evening performances (180Kč) by the **Křižík Fountain** dancing fountains devised for the 1891 Exhibition by the Czech inventor František Křižík. Call ☏220 103 224 or visit Ⓦwww.krizikovafontana.cz for details of performances.

Lapidárium

Výstaviště 422 ☏233 375 636, Ⓦwww.nm.cz. Tues–Fri noon–6pm, Sat & Sun 10am–6pm. 40Kč.
Official depository for the city's sculptures which are under threat either from demolition or from the weather, the Lapidárium houses a much overlooked collection, ranging from the eleventh to the nineteenth century. Some of the statues saved from the perils of Prague's polluted atmosphere, such as the bronze equestrian statue of St George, will be familiar if you've visited Prague Castle; others, such as the figures from the towers of the Charles Bridge, are more difficult to inspect closely in their original sites. Many of the original statues from the bridge can be seen here, as well as the ones that were fished out of the Vltava after the flood of 1890.

One of the most outstanding sights is what remains of the Krocín fountain, a highly ornate Renaissance work in red marble, which used to grace Staroměstské náměstí (see

PLACES

Holešovice

Getting to Troja and the Zoo

To reach Troja and the Zoo you can either walk from Výstaviště, catch bus #112, which runs frequently from metro Nádraží Holešovice, or take a boat (April to Oct 3–4 daily; 120Kč; ⓦ www.paroplavba.cz) from the PPS landing place on Rašínovo nábřeží, metro Karlovo náměstí – see map on p.104.

p.76). Several pompous imperial monuments that were bundled into storage after the demise of the Habsburgs in 1918 round off the museum's collection. By far the most impressive is the bronze statue of Marshal Radecký, scourge of the 1848 revolution, carried aloft on a shield by eight Habsburg soldiers.

Stromovka

Originally laid out as hunting grounds for the noble occupants of the Castle, Stromovka is now Prague's largest and leafiest public park. If you're heading north for Troja and the city zoo, a stroll through the park is by far the most pleasant approach. If you want to explore a little more of the park, head west sticking to the park's southern border and you'll eventually come to a neo-Gothic former royal hunting chateau, which served as the seat of the Governor of Bohemia until 1918.

Troja Chateau (Trojský zámek)

U trojského zámku 1. April–Sept Tues–Sun 10am–6pm; Nov–March Sat & Sun 10am–5pm. 100Kč. The Troja Chateau was designed by Jean-Baptiste Mathey for the powerful Šternberg family towards the end of the seventeenth century. The best features of the rusty-red Baroque facade are the monumental balustrades, where blackened figures of giants and titans battle it out. The star exhibits of the interior are the gushing frescoes depicting

the victories of the Habsburg Emperor Leopold I (who reigned from 1657 to 1705) over the Turks, which cover every inch of the walls and ceilings of the grand hall. You also get to wander through the chateau's pristine, trend-setting, French-style formal gardens, the first of their kind in Bohemia.

▲ STROSSMAYEROVO

Prague Zoo

U trojského zámku 3 ⓦ www.zoopraha. cz. Daily: March 9am–5pm; April, May, Sept & Oct 9am–6pm; June–Aug 9am–7pm; Nov–Feb 9am–4pm. 100Kč. Founded in 1931 on the site of one of Troja's numerous hillside vineyards, Prague's zoo has had a lot of money poured into it and now has some very imaginative enclosures. All the usual animals are on show here – including elephants, hippos, giraffes, zebras, big cats and bears – and kids, at least, will enjoy themselves. A bonus in the summer is the fact you can take a chairlift (*lanová dráha*) from the duck pond over the enclosures to the top of the hill, where the prize exhibits – a rare breed of miniature horse known as Przewalski – hang out. Other highlights include the red pandas, the giant tortoises, the Komodo dragons and the bats that actually fly past your face in the Twilight Zone.

Botanic Gardens

Nádvorní 134 ⓦ www.botanicka.cz. Daily: March & Oct 9am–5pm; April 9am–6pm; May–Sept 9am–7pm; Nov–Feb 9am–4pm. 100Kč. Another reason for coming out to Troja is to visit the city's botanic gardens, hidden in the woods to the north of the chateau. The botanic gardens feature a vineyard, a Japanese garden, several glasshouses and great views over Prague. Hidden in the woods a little higher up the hill, there's also a spectacular, new, curvaceous greenhouse, **Fata Morgana** (same hours but closed Mon), with butterflies flitting about amid the desert and tropical plants. Be warned that the Fata Morgana – which means "mirage" in Czech – is very popular and there are vast queues at the weekend.

Shops

Pivní galerie

U Průhonu 9. Mon–Fri 11am–8pm. The largest selection of bottled Czech beers in the capital (all at under 30Kč a throw), which you can drink in the shop or take away.

Cafés

Delicatesse

Kostelní 16 ⓦ www.delicatesse.cz. Daily 9am–9pm. French bakery serving hot and cold sandwiches, quiches and pastries; they also deliver.

Orange

Puškinovo naměstí 13. Mon–Sat 10am–11pm, Sun 11am–3pm. Trendy, brightly decorated café with seats outside overlooking a quiet residential square and good pasta dishes, bruschetta snacks, fresh juices and ice cream.

Restaurants

Hanavský pavilón

Letenské sady 173 ☎ 233 323 641, ⓦ www.hanavskypavilon.cz. Highly ornate wrought-iron Art Nouveau pleasure pavilion high above the Vltava, with stunning views; Czech and international mains 550–750Kč.

La Bistrot de Marlène

Schwaigerova 3 ☎ 224 921 853, ⓦ www.bistrotdemarlene.cz. Mon–Fri noon–2.30pm & 7–10.30pm, Sat 7–10.30pm. Really excellent French cuisine, with exceptional service, in a stylish, formal restaurant housed in a villa. Mains around 500–600Kč.

La Crêperie

Janovského 4 ☎ 220 878 040. Mon–Sat 11am–11pm, Sun 11am–10pm. Stylish but inexpensive French-run crêperie serving sweet and savoury pancakes, French liqueurs and the rare Nová Paka beer.

Svatá Klara (Saint Clare)

U Trojského zámku 35 ☎ 233 540 173, ⓦ www.svataclara.cz. Daily

7pm–1am. Formal, evening-only restaurant, first opened in 1679, in a romantic wine cave setting near the zoo. Specializes in fondues and Czech game dishes from 500Kč.

Pubs

Fraktal
Šmeralova 1. Daily 11am–1am. Very popular expat cellar bar with ad hoc furnishings, exhibitions and occasional live music.

Letenský zámeček
Letenské sady ⓦ www. letenskyzamecek.cz. Daily 11am– 11.30pm. The beer garden, with its great views down the Vltava, is popular with the locals; the *Ullman* restaurant inside is much more upmarket, and serves upgraded Czech cuisine.

U houbaře (The Mushroom)
Dukelských hrdinů 30. Daily 11am–midnight. Comfortable pub, directly opposite the Veletržní Palace, serving Pilsner Urquell and pub food.

Clubs

Mecca
U Průhonu 3 ⓦ www.mecca.cz. Café/ restaurant: Mon–Thurs 10am–11pm, Fri & Sat 10am–6am; club: Mon–Thurs 8pm–2am, Fri & Sat 8pm–6am. Despite being out in Prague 7, this coolly converted factory is one of the most impressive, professional and popular clubs in Prague.

Accommodation

Hotels and pensions

Compared to the price of almost everything else in Prague, accommodation is very expensive. If you're looking for a double and can pay around 4000Kč (£100/$190) a night then you'll find plenty of choice. At the other end of the scale, there are numerous hostels charging as little as 400Kč (£10/$19) for a bed. However, there's a chronic shortage of decent, inexpensive to middle-range places. One way round this is to search the Internet for special offers or for self-catering apartments, either of which usually considerably undercuts the exorbitant rack rates.

All accommodation prices in this chapter are for the cheapest double room in high season (April–Oct). All rooms are en suite and breakfast is included unless otherwise stated.

Hradčany

Domus Henrici Loretánská 11 ☎220 511 369, ⓦwww.domus-henrici.cz. Stylish, discreet hotel in a fab location, with just eight rooms/apartments, some with splendid views. Run in conjunction with *Domus Balthasar* on Mostecká, by the Charles Bridge. Doubles from 4800Kč.

Questenberk Úvoz 5 ☎220 407 600, ⓦwww.questenberk.cz. From the outside, this hotel looks like a Baroque chapel, but inside it's been totally modernized. Rooms are smart but plain for the price, though the views from some are superb. Doubles from 5000Kč.

U krále Karla (King Charles) Úvoz 4 ☎234 125 229, ⓦwww.romantikhotels. com. Possibly the most tastefully exquisite of all the small luxury hotels in the castle district, with beautiful antique furnishings and stained-glass windows. It's situated just at the top of Nerudova, a fair walk from the nearest tram stop. Doubles from 5500Kč.

U zlatého koníčka (Golden Horse) Úvoz 8 ☎603 841 790, ⓦwww.goldenhorse. cz. Small, plain, clean, en-suite rooms at

Booking accommodation

Prague can be pretty busy all year round, so it's as well to book in advance either directly with the hotels or through one of the accommodation agencies listed below. **High season** runs from April to October, while prices are at their very highest over New Year, but drop by as much as a third in July and August, and sometimes by half in the **low season** in February and November.

If you arrive in Prague without having booked a room, there are several **accommodation agencies**, most of which can book you into either a hotel or pension; some can also help you find a hostel bed or a private room in an apartment. Before agreeing to part with any money, be sure you know exactly where you're staying and check about transport to the centre – some places can be a long way out of town. The largest agency in Prague is **AVE** (☎251 551 011, ⓦwww.avetravel.cz), who have desks at the airport, both international train stations, and several points throughout the city; they can book anything from hostels to hotels and are therefore a good last-minute fall-back. Another option is **Pragotur** (☎221 714 130, ⓦwww.prague-info.cz), who have desks in various PIS tourist offices. They too can book anything from hotels to hostels, but they specialize in private rooms.

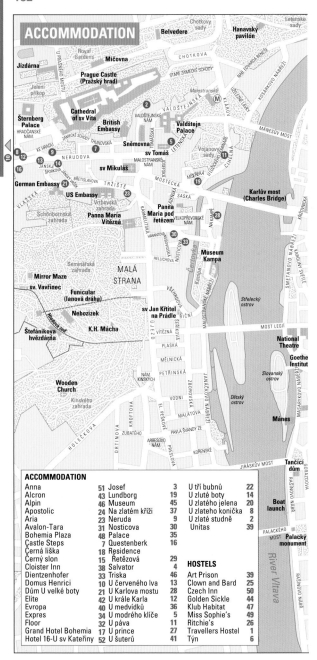

ACCOMMODATION

Belvedere

Hanavský pavilón

Letenské sady

Royal Gardens

Míčovna

Jízdárna

Prague Castle (Pražský hrad)

CHOTKOVA

STARÉ ZÁMECKÉ SCHODY

Jelení příkop

Cathedral of sv Víta

Šternberg Palace

HRADČANSKÉ NÁM.

British Embassy

VALDŠTEJNSKÁ

Valdštejn Palace

Valdštejn Palace

Sněmovna

sv Tomáš

KE HRADU

ZÁMECKÉ SCHODY THUNOVSKÁ

NERUDOVA

sv Mikuláš

JÁNSKÁ ŠPORKOVA

BŘETISLAVOVA

MALOSTRANSKÉ NÁM.

Vojanovy sady

German Embassy

US Embassy

Vrtbovská zahrada

MOSTECKÁ

TRŽIŠTĚ

SASKÁ

Karlův most (Charles Bridge)

Schönbornská zahrada

Panna Maria Vítězná

Panna Maria pod řetězem

VELKOPŘEVORSKÉ NÁM.

NA KAMPĚ

HARANTOVA

Seminářská zahrada

MALÁ STRANA

HELLICHOVA

Museum Kampa

Kampa

Mirror Maze

sv Vavřinec

Funicular (lanová dráha)

Nebozizek

Hladová zeď

Štefánikova hvězdárna

K.H. Mácha

VŠEHRDOVA

sv Jan Křtitel na Prádle

ŘÍČNÍ

VÍTĚZNÁ

Střelecký ostrov

MOST LEGII

PLASKÁ

National Theatre

MĚLNICKÁ

Goethe Institut

PETŘÍNSKÁ

Slovanský ostrov

Wooden Church

NÁM. KINSKÝCH

Kinského zahrada

VODNI

EL. PEŠNOVÉ

MALÁTOVA

Dětský ostrov

Mánes

HOLEČKOVA

DRTINOVA

ZUBATÉHO

KROFTOVA

ARBESOVO NÁM.

PREŠOVÁ

PAVLA ŠVANDY ZE

KOŘENSKÉ

JIRÁSKŮV MOST

Tančící dům

RAŠÍNOVO NÁBŘEŽÍ

Boat launch

PALACKÉHO MOST

Palacký monument

River Vltava

RAŠÍNOVO NÁBŘEŽÍ

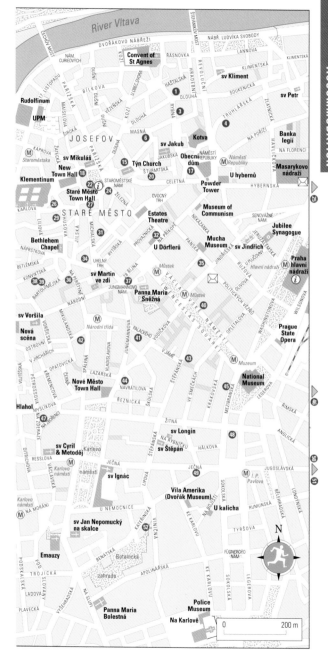

real bargain prices in a perfect location on the way up to the Hrad. Breakfast in the brick-vaulted cellar is an extra 100Kč. Doubles from 1650Kč.

Malá Strana

Aria Tržiště 9 ☎225 334 111, ⓦwww.ariahotel.net. Prague's first real stab at a boutique hotel, this superbly stylish, contemporary place has a stunning roof terrace and music-themed floors (and rooms) from jazz and rock to classical and opera. Doubles from 10,000Kč.

Castle Steps Nerudova 10 ☎257 216 337, ⓦwww.castlesteps.com; UK ☎0800/883 0467; US & Canada ☎1-800/860 0571. This is without doubt Malá Strana's most amazing bargain, with a variety of beautifully furnished rooms and apartments, some with unbelievable views, others with self-catering facilities. There's no reception as such, but breakfast is served in a cellar (with free Internet access) on Úvoz until 11am. Doubles from 2000Kč.

Dientzenhofer Nosticova 2 ☎257 316 830, ⓦwww.dientzenhofer.cz. Birthplace of the eponymous architect Kilian Ignác Dientzenhofer and a very popular and unpretentious pension due to the fact that it's one of the few reasonably priced places (anywhere in Prague) to have wheelchair access. Doubles from 3200Kč.

Dům U velké boty (The Big Shoe) Vlašská 30 ☎257 532 088, ⓦwww.dumuvelkeboty.cz. The sheer discreetness of this pension, in a lovely old building in the quiet backstreets, is one of its main draws. Run by a very friendly couple, who speak good English, it has a series of characterful, tastefully modernized rooms, some en suite, some not. Breakfast is extra, but worth it. Doubles from 3000Kč.

Lundborg Lužického semináře 3 ☎257 011 911, ⓦwww.lundborg.cz. Very stylish Swedish-run apartment suites with Baroque painted ceilings and tasteful furnishings, as well as Jacuzzis and Internet access in every room. It is in the thick of it, however, right by the Charles Bridge tower, and therefore could be noisy. Suites from 4250Kč.

Neruda Nerudova 44 ☎257 535 557, ⓦwww.hotelneruda-praha.cz. Stylish hotel a fair walk up Nerudova, with a funky, glass-roofed foyer, lots of natural stone, and smart, minimalist modern decor in the rooms. Doubles from 5700Kč.

Nosticova Nosticova 1 ☎257 312 513, ⓦwww.nosticova.com. Baroque house with ten beautifully restored apartments replete with antique furnishings, sumptuous bathrooms and small kitchens, on a peaceful square not far from the Charles Bridge. Apartments from 7500Kč.

U červeného Iva (Red Lion) Nerudova 41 ☎257 533 832, ⓦwww.hotelredlion.cz. The decor here is outstanding: original seventeenth-century wooden ceilings throughout, complemented by tasteful furnishings, parquet flooring and rugs; the service less so. Doubles from 6300Kč.

U Karlova mostu Na Kampě 15 ☎257 531 430, ⓦwww.archibald.cz. Situated on a lovely tree-lined square, just off the Charles Bridge, the rooms in this former brewery (now a pub-restaurant) have real character, despite the modern fittings. Doubles from 5500Kč.

U modrého klíče (Blue Key) Letenská 14 ☎257 534 361, ⓦwww.bluekey.cz. Friendly, swish, blue-themed hotel in a good location (despite the busy road outside), just a short stroll from Malostranské náměstí; ask for a room facing into the lovely courtyard. Doubles from 3000Kč.

U páva (The Peacock) U lužického semináře 32 ☎257 532 269, ⓦwww.romantichotels.cz/upava. Tucked away in the quiet backstreets, U páva boasts some sumptuously over-the-top Baroque fittings real and repro. Some rooms have views over to the castle and service is good. Doubles from 6200Kč.

U zlaté studně (The Golden well) U zlaté studně 4 ☎257 011 213, ⓦwww.goldenwellhotel.com. The location is pretty special: tucked into the terraces below Prague Castle, next to the terraced gardens, with incredible views across the rooftops. The rooms aren't half bad either, with lots of original ceilings, and there's a good restaurant attached, with a wonderful summer terrace. Doubles from 6400Kč.

U zluté boty **Jánský vršek 11** ☎257 532 269, ✉www.zlutabota.cz. Hidden away in a lovely old backstreet, this Baroque hotel has real character, with the odd original ceiling, exposed beams and, in one room, a ceramic stove and authentic wood-panelling. Doubles from 3700Kč.

Staré Město

Apostolic **Staroměstské náměstí 26** ☎221 632 222, ✉www.prague-residence.cz. If you want a room overlooking the astronomical clock on Old Town Square, then book in here, well in advance. There are beautiful antique furnishings, big oak ceilings, but only a very few rooms, including a single, as well an attic suite for four. Doubles from 6400Kč.

Avalon-Tara **Havelská 15** ☎224 228 083, ✉www.prague-hotel.ws. Perfect location right over the market on Havelská, with seven very small, very simply furnished, but clean, rooms, with or without en-suite facilities. Doubles from 2200Kč.

Černá liška (The Black Fox) **Mikulášská 2** ☎224 232 250, ✉www.cernaliska. cz. Well-appointed rooms, all with lovely wooden floors, some with incredible views onto Old Town Square, quieter ones at the back. Doubles from 4850Kč.

Černý slon (Black Elephant) **Týnská 1** ☎222 321 521, ✉www.hotelcernyslon. cz. Another ancient building tucked away off Old Town Square by the north portal of the Týn church, now tastefully converted into a very comfortable hotel. Doubles from 3500Kč.

Cloister Inn **Konviktská 14** ☎224 211 020, ✉www.cloister-inn.com. Pleasant, well-equipped hotel housed in a nunnery in one of the backstreets; the rooms are basic, but the location is good. There are even cheaper rooms in the *Pension Unitas* in the same building (see below). Doubles from 4000Kč.

Expres **Skořepka 5** ☎224 211 801, ✉www.hotel-expres.com. Friendly little hotel with few pretensions: basic fittings, low prices and an excellent location right in the centre of Staré Město. Doubles from 1600Kč.

Grand Hotel Bohemia **Kralodvorská 4** ☎234 608 111, ✉www.grandhotel-bohemia.cz. Probably the most elegant luxury hotel in the old town, just behind the Obecní dům, with some very tasty Art Nouveau decor and all the amenities you'd expect from an Austrian outfit. Doubles from 5000Kč.

Josef **Rybná 20** ☎221 700 901, ✉www. hoteljosef.com. Prague's top designer hotel exudes modern professionalism, the lobby is a symphony in off-white efficiency and the rooms continue the crisply maintained minimalist theme. Doubles from 5000Kč.

Residence Řetězová **Řetězová 9** ☎222 221 800, ✉www.residenceretezova. com. Characterful apartments of all sizes, with a kitchenette, wooden or stone floors, Gothic vaulting or wooden beams and repro furnishings throughout. Apartments from 4500Kč.

U medvídků (The Little Bears) **Na Perštýně 7** ☎224 211 916, ✉www. umedvidku.cz. The rooms above this famous Prague pub are plainly furnished, quiet considering the locale, and therefore something of an old town bargain; booking ahead essential. Doubles from 3000Kč.

U prince **Staroměstské náměstí 29** ☎224 213 807, ✉www.hoteluprince. cz. Plush hotel, situated right on Old Town Square, with lots of original wooden ceilings and views across to the astronomical clock. This is not a place for those who want to lose the crowds, as they're standing right outside your door, but if you want to be central, look no further. Doubles from 6000Kč.

U tří bubnů (The Three Drums) **U radnice 10/14** ☎224 214 855, ✉www. utribubnu.cz. Small hotel of Old Town Square with five tastefully furnished rooms, either with original fifteenth-century wooden ceilings or lots of exposed beams. Doubles from 3700Kč.

Unitas **Bartolomějská 9** ☎224 230 603, ✉www.unitas.cz. Set in a Franciscan nunnery, the *Unitas* offers both simple twins and bargain dorm beds in its "Art Prison Hostel", converted secret police prison cells (Havel stayed in P6). No smoking or drinking, but unbelievably cheap. Twins from 1580Kč.

U zlatého jelena (The Golden Stag) Štupartská 6 ☎ 222 317 237, ⊛ www. hotel-u-zlateho-jelena.cz. Inexpensive little pension with spacious rooms very simply furnished with parquet flooring and repro ironwork. Doubles from 3600Kč.

Nové Město

Alcron Štěpánská 40 ☎ 222 820 000, ⊛ www.radisson.com. Giant 1930s luxury hotel, just off Wenceslas Square, which has been superbly restored to its former Art Deco glory by the Radisson SAS chain. Double rooms here are without doubt the most luxurious and tasteful you'll find in Nové Město. Doubles from 5000Kč.

Bohemia Plaza Žitná 50 ☎ 224 941 000, ⊛ www.bohemiaplaza.com. Big, patrician, family-run hotel with themed rooms, some stuffed with antiques, others with tasteful repro and more modern gear. Doubles from 3400Kč.

Elite Ostrovní 32 ☎ 224 932 250, ⊛ www.hotelelite.cz. An efficient, stylish and very centrally located hotel with its own underground car park, occupying an ancient building at heart, with an enclosed courtyard and the odd Renaissance feature retained. Doubles from 3700Kč.

Evropa Václavské náměstí 25 ☎ 224 215 387, ⊛ www.evropahotel.cz. Potentially the most beautiful hotel in Prague, built in the 1900s and sumptuously decorated in Art Nouveau style. Yet despite its prime location and its incredible decor, this place is still run like an old Communist behemoth – a blast from the past in every sense. The rooms are furnished in repro Louis XIV, and there are some cheaper ones without en-suite facilities. Doubles from 1950Kč.

Floor Na příkopě 13 ☎ 234 076 300, ⊛ www.floorhotel.cz. Situated right on one of Prague's premier pedestrianized shopping streets, on the edge of the Staré Město, this comfortable hotel goes for a predominantly modern look. Doubles from 3000Kč.

Hotel 16 – U sv Kateřiny Kateřinská 16 ☎ 224 920 636, ⊛ www.hotel16.cz. Really friendly, family-run hotel offering small, plain but clean en-suite rooms. There's a small terraced garden at the back and botanic gardens nearby. Doubles from 3500Kč.

Museum Mezibranská 15 ☎ 296 325 186, ⊛ www.pension-museum.cz. Although situated on one of the busiest roads in Prague, right by the National Museum, the plain, budget-priced modern rooms in this pension all face onto a quiet courtyard. Doubles from 3000Kč.

Na zlatém křiži (Golden cross) Jungmannovo náměstí 2 ☎ 224 245 419, ⊛ www.goldencross.cz. Small hotel in a very tall (no lift), narrow building just a step away from the bottom of Wenceslas Square. Rooms are spacious – especially the suites – and decked out in tasteful repro furnishings with nice parquet floors. Doubles from 3000Kč.

Palace Panská 12 ☎ 224 093 181, ⊛ www.palacehotel.cz. Luxury hotel just off Wenceslas Square, renowned for its excellent service and facilities – a solid choice. Doubles from 5000Kč.

Salvator Truhlářská 10 ☎ 222 312 234, ⊛ www.salvator.cz. Very good location for the price, just a minute's walk from náměstí Republiky, with small but clean rooms (the cheaper ones without en-suite facilities), and a sports bar on the ground floor; advance booking advisable. Doubles from 2100Kč.

U šuterů Palackého 4 ☎ 224 948 235, ⊛ www.usuteru.cz. Fin-de-siècle furnishings, parquet flooring, vaulted ceilings and a decent location between Národní and Wenceslas Square make this small pension pretty good value. Doubles from 3000Kč.

Vinohrady & Žižkov

Alpin Velehradská 25 ☎ 222 723 551, ⊛ www.alpin.cz. Clean, bare, bargain rooms on the border between Vinohrady and Žižkov. Doubles from 1650Kč.

Anna Budečská 17, Vinohrady ☎ 222 513 111, ⊛ www.hotelanna.cz. Plain, bright white rooms, warm friendly staff and a decent location make this a popular choice in Prague 2. Doubles from 3000Kč.

Triška Vinohradská 105 ☎ 222 727 313, ⊛ www.hotel-triska.cz. Large fin-de-siècle hotel with comfortable rooms and parquet floors; they've made an effort with the interior decor, the service is good and it's close to the metro. Doubles from 2300Kč.

Hostels

Art Prison Bartolomějská 9, Staré Město 9 ☎224 230 603, ⊛www.unitas.cz; metro Národní třída. Set in a Franciscan nunnery and part of *Pension Unitas*, this hostel offers both simple twins and bargain dorm beds in converted secret police prison cells (Havel was kept in P6). No smoking or drinking. Twins from 1580Kč.

Clown and Bard Bořivojova 102, Žižkov ☎222 716 453, ⊛www.clownandbard. com. Žižkov hostel that's so laid-back it's horizontal, and not a place to go if you don't like hippies. Nevertheless, it's clean, undeniably cheap, stages events and has laundry facilities. Doubles from 1000Kč, dorm beds from 300Kč.

Czech Inn Francouzská 76, Vinohrady ☎267 267 600, ⊛www.czech-inn.com. Upbeat, designer hostel that feels and looks like a hotel, with friendly and helpful staff and a choice of dormitories and private rooms. Doubles from 1600Kč; dorm beds from 390Kč.

Golden Sickle Vodičkova 10, Nové Město ☎222 230 773, ⊛www.golden-sickle.com. Clean, modern, friendly hostel with fittings from IKEA and a great central courtyard. Breakfast included. Dorm beds from 450Kč; doubles from 1400Kč.

Klub Habitat Na Zderaze 10, Nové Město ☎233 920 118, ⊛www.klub-habitat.cz. Perfectly serviceable hostel in a great location south of Národní. Book ahead. Dorm beds from 450Kč.

Miss Sophie's Melounová 3, Nové Město ☎296 303 530, ⊛www.miss-sophies. com. The most central of Prague's smart new designer hostels offering everything from cheap dorm beds to fully equipped apartments. Dorm beds from 400Kč; doubles from 1790Kč.

Ritchie's Karlova 9 & 13, Staré Město ☎222 221 229, ⊛www.ritchieshostel. cz. In the midst of the human river that is Karlova, this Old Town hostel has no in-house laundry or cooking facilities, but it's clean and accommodation ranges from en-suite doubles to twelve-bed dorms. Doubles from 1650Kč, dorm beds 330Kč.

Travellers Hostel Dlouhá 33, Staré Město ☎224 826 662, ⊛www .travellers.cz. Very centrally located party hostel (although it's not the cleanest of places), situated above the *Roxy* nightclub, and the main booking office for a network of hostels – if there's not enough room here, staff will find you a bed in one of their other central branches. Dorm beds from 400Kč; doubles from 1300Kč.

Týn Týnská 19, Staré Město ☎224 808 333, ⊛www.hosteltyn.web2001.cz. Prague's most centrally located hostel, just metres from Old Town Square. Doubles from 1200Kč, six-bed dorms 400Kč.

Essentials

Arrival

Prague is one of Europe's smaller capital cities, with a population of around one and a quarter million. The airport lies just over 10km northwest of the city centre, with only a bus link or taxi to get you into town. By contrast, both the international train stations and the main bus terminal are linked to the centre by the fast and efficient metro system.

By plane

Prague's **Ruzyně** airport (☎ 220 113 314, ⓦ www.prg.aero) is connected to the city by minibus, bus and taxi. The Cedaz (ⓦ www.cedaz.cz) shared **minibus service** will take you (and several others) to your hotel for around 360Kč. The minibus also runs a scheduled service (daily 5.30am–9.30pm; every 30min), which stops first at Dejvická metro station, at the end of metro line A (journey time 20min), and ends up at náměstí Republiky (journey time 30min); the full journey currently costs 120Kč. Another option is the **Prague Airport Shuttle** (ⓦ www.prague-airport-shuttle. com) which will take you into town for 600Kč for up to four passengers.

The cheapest way to get into town is on **local bus #119** (daily 5am to midnight; every 15–20min; journey time 20min), which stops frequently and also ends its journey outside Dejvická metro station. You can buy your ticket from the public transport (DP) information desk in arrivals (daily 7am–10pm), or from the nearby machines or newsagents. If you're going to use public transport

whilst in Prague, you might as well buy a pass straight away (see p.142). If you arrive between midnight and 5am, you can catch the hourly night bus #510 to Divoká Šárka, the terminus for night tram #51, which will take you on to Národní in the centre of town.

If you're thinking of taking a **taxi** from the airport into the centre, choose AAA Taxi (☎ 14014, ⓦ www.aaataxi.cz), as Prague taxi drivers have a reputation for overcharging. AAA have a rank outside arrivals and the journey to the city centre should cost around 400–500Kč.

By train and bus

International trains arrive either at Praha hlavní nádraží, on the edge of Nové Město and Vinohrady, or at Praha-Holešovice, which lies in an industrial suburb north of the city centre. At both stations you'll find exchange outlets, 24-hour left-luggage offices (*úschovna zavazadel*) and accommodation agencies (plus a tourist office at Hlavní nádraží). Both stations are on metro lines (see flap map), and Hlavní nádraží is only a five-minute walk from Václavské náměstí (Wenceslas Square).

Prague's main **bus terminal** is Praha-Florenc (metro Florenc), on the eastern edge of Nové Město, where virtually all long-distance international and domestic services terminate. It's a confusing place to end up, but it has a left-luggage office upstairs (daily 5am–11pm), and you can make a quick exit to the adjacent metro station.

City transport

The centre of Prague, where most of the city's sights are concentrated, is reasonably small and best explored on foot. At some point, however, in order to cross the city quickly or reach some of the more widely dispersed attractions, you'll need to use the city's cheap and efficient **public transport system** (*dopravní podnik* or DP; ⓦ www.dpp .cz), which comprises the metro and a network of trams and buses. You can get free maps, tickets and passes from the DP information offices at both airport terminals (daily 7am–10pm), from Holešovice train station (Mon–Fri 7am–6pm), Můstek metro (Mon–Fri 7am–6pm), Muzeum metro (daily 7am–9pm) and Anděl metro (Mon–Fri 7am–6pm).

Tickets and passes

Most Praguers simply buy monthly passes, and to avoid having to understand the complexities of the single ticket system, you too are best off buying a travel pass.

You can buy a **travel pass** (*časová jízdenka*) for 24 hours (*na 24 hodin*; 100Kč), three days (*na 3 dní*; 330Kč), or five days (*na 5 dní*; 500Kč); no photos or ID are needed, though you must write your name and date of birth on the reverse of the ticket, and punch it to validate when you first use it. All the passes are available from DP outlets, and the 24-hour pass is also available from ticket machines.

Probably the single most daunting aspect of buying a ticket is having to use the **ticket machines**, found inside all metro stations and at some bus and tram stops. Despite the multitude of buttons on the machines, for a single **ticket** (*lístek* or *jízdenka*) in the two central zones (2 *pásma*), there are just two basic choices. The 18Kč version (*zlevněná*) allows you to travel for up to fifteen minutes on the trams or buses, or up to four stops on the metro; it's known as a *nepřestupní jízdenka*, or "no change ticket", although you can in fact change metro lines (but not buses or trams). The 26Kč version (*plnocenná*) is valid for one hour at **peak times** (Mon–Fri 5am–8pm) – or an hour and a half off-peak – during which you may change trams, buses or metro lines as many times as you like, hence its name, *přestupní jízdenka*, or "changing ticket". Half-price tickets are available for children aged 6–15; under-6s travel free.

If you're buying a ticket from one of the machines, you must press the appropriate button – press it once for one ticket, twice for two and so on – followed by the *výdej*/enter button, after which you put your money in. The machines do give change, but if you don't have enough coins, you may find the person on duty in the metro office by the barriers can give you change or sell you a ticket. Tickets can also be bought, en masse, and rather more easily, from a tobacconist (*tabák*), street kiosk, newsagent, PIS office or any place that displays the yellow DP sticker. When you enter the metro, or board a tram or bus, you must validate your ticket by validating it in one of the electronic machines to hand.

There's nothing to stop people from freeloading on the system of course, since there are no barriers. However, plain-clothes **inspectors** (*revizoři*) make random checks and will issue an on-the-spot fine of 500Kč (950Kč if you don't cough up immediately) to anyone caught without a valid ticket or pass; controllers should show you their ID (a small metal disc) and give you a receipt (*paragon*).

Metro

Prague's futuristic, Soviet-built **metro** is fast, smooth and ultra-clean, running daily from 5am to midnight with trains

The Prague Card

For those coming for a long weekend, it's worth considering buying the **Prague Card** (ⓦwww.praguecard.biz), which is valid for four days and gives free entry into over fifty sights within the city for 790Kč, plus another 330Kč for a travel pass. The one major omission is that the card doesn't include the sights of the Jewish Museum. All in all, the card will save you a lot of hassle, but not necessarily that much money. The card is available from all travel information and PIS offices (see p.144).

every two minutes during peak hours, slowing down to every four to ten minutes by late evening. Its three lines intersect at various points in the city centre and the route plans are easy to follow (see the colour map at the back of the book).

The stations are fairly discreetly marked above ground with the metro logo, in green (line A), yellow (line B) or red (line C). The constant bleeping at metro entrances is to enable blind people to locate the escalators, which are a free-for-all, with no fast lane. Once inside the metro, it's worth knowing that *výstup* means exit and *přestup* will lead you to one of the connecting lines at an interchange. The digital clock at the end of the platform tells you what time it is and how long it was since the last train.

Trams

The electric **tram** (*tramvaj*) **system**, in operation since 1891, negotiates Prague's hills and cobbles with remarkable dexterity. Modern rolling stock is gradually being introduced, but most of Prague's trams (traditionally red, but often now plastered over with advertising) date back to the Communist era. After the metro, trams are the fastest and most efficient way of getting around, running every six to eight minutes at peak times, and every five to fifteen minutes at other times – check the timetables posted at every stop (*zastávka*), which list the departure times from that specific stop. Note that it is the custom for younger folk (and men of all ages) to vacate their seat when an older woman enters the carriage.

Tram #22, which runs from Vinohrady to Hradčany via the centre of town and

Malá Strana, is a good way to get to grips with the lie of the land, and a cheap way of sightseeing, though you should beware of pickpockets. From Easter to October, interwar **tram #91** runs from Výstaviště to náměstí Republiky via Malá Strana (Sat & Sun hourly noon–6pm) and back again; the ride takes forty minutes and costs 25Kč. **Night trams** (*noční tramvaje*; #51–58) run roughly every thirty to forty minutes from around midnight to 4.30am; the routes are different from the daytime ones, though at some point all night trams pass along Lazarská in Nové Město.

For more tram routes, see the colour map at the back of the book.

Buses

You'll rarely need to get on a **bus** (*autobus*) within Prague itself, since most of them keep well out of the centre of town. If you're intent upon visiting the zoo or staying in some of the city's more obscure suburbs though, you may need to use them: their hours of operation are similar to those of the trams (though generally less frequent). **Night buses** (*noční autobusy*) run just once an hour between midnight and 5am.

Boats

In the summer months there's a regular **boat service** on the River Vltava run by the PPS (*Pražská paroplavební společnost*; ☎ 224 930 017, ⓦ www.paroplavba. cz) from just south of Jiráskův most on Rašínovo nábřeží (see map on p.104). In the summer three or four boats a day run to Troja (see p.126) in the northern suburbs (May to mid-Sept daily; April & mid-Sept to Oct Sat & Sun only; 200Kč return).

In addition, the PPS also offers **boat trips** around Prague (April to mid-Sept daily 1–2hr; 190–290Kč) on board a 1930s paddlesteamer. Another option is to hop aboard the much smaller boats run by Prague-Venice (℡ 603 819 947, ⓦ www.prazskebenatky.cz), which depart for a half-hour meander over to the Čertovka by Kampa island (300Kč). The boats depart from the north side of the Charles Bridge on the Staré Město bank.

Taxis

Taxis come in all shapes and sizes, and, theoretically at least, are extremely cheap. However, if they think they can get away with it, many Prague taxi drivers will attempt to overcharge; the worst offenders, needless to say, hang out at the taxi ranks closest to the tourist sights. Officially, the initial fare on the meter should be around 40Kč plus 28Kč per kilometre within Prague. The best advice is to have your hotel or pension call you one – you then qualify for a cheaper rate – rather than hail one or pick one up at the taxi ranks. The cab company with the best reputation is AAA Taxi (℡ 14014, ⓦ www.aaataxi.cz), which has metered taxis all over Prague.

Information

In Prague, the main **tourist office** is the **Prague Information Service** or **PIS** (Pražská informační služba), whose main branch is within the Staroměstská radnice on Staroměstské náměstí (April–Oct Mon–Fri 9am–7pm, Sat & Sun 9am–6pm; Nov–March Mon–Fri 9am–6pm, Sat & Sun 9am–5pm; ⓦ www.prague-info.cz). There are additional PIS offices at Rytířská 31, Staré Město (metro Můstek), in the main train station, Praha hlavní nádraží, plus an (April–Oct only)

office in the Malá Strana bridge tower on the Charles Bridge. PIS staff speak English, but their helpfulness varies enormously; however, they can usually answer most enquiries, and can organize accommodation, sell maps, guides and theatre tickets.

PIS also distributes and sells some useful **listings** publications, including *Culture in Prague/Česká kultura* (ⓦ www.ceskakultura.cz), a monthly English-language booklet listing the major events,

Websites

Maps ⓦ www.mapy.cz. This site will provide you with a thumbnail map to help you find any hotel, restaurant, pub, shop or street in Prague (and elsewhere in the Czech Republic).

Prague TV ⓦ www.prague.tv. Not in fact a TV station at all, but an online Prague information, listings and news service, updated daily.

Radio Prague ⓦ www.radio.cz/english. An informative site with the latest news and weather as audio or text.

Welcome to the Czech Republic ⓦ www.czech.cz. Basic information on the country in English, and on the worldwide network of Czech Centres, run by the Czech Foreign Ministry.

concerts and exhibitions; *Přehled*, a more comprehensive monthly listings magazine (in Czech only); and the weekly **English-language paper**, *Prague Post* (🌐 www.praguepost.com), which carries selective listings on the latest exhibitions, shows, gigs and events around the capital.

The PIS also sells the useful **Prague Card** (see box on p.143).

Festivals and events

Masopust (Shrove Tuesday)
The approach of Masopust (the Czech version of Mardi Gras) prompts a five-day programme of parties, concerts and parades, centred on the Žižkov district of Prague; 🌐 www.carnevale.cz.

Easter (Velikonoce)
The age-old sexist ritual of whipping girls' calves with braided birch twigs tied together with ribbons (*pomlázky*) is still practised. To prevent such a fate, the girls are supposed to offer the boys a coloured Easter egg and pour a bucket of cold water over them.

"Burning of the Witches" (pálení čarodějnic)
Halloween comes early to the Czech Republic when bonfires are lit across the country, and old brooms thrown out and burned on April 30, as everyone celebrates the end of the long winter.

Prague Spring Festival (Pražské jaro)
By far the biggest annual arts event and the country's most prestigious international music festival. Established in 1946, it traditionally begins on May 12, the anniversary of Smetana's death, with a procession from his grave in Vyšehrad to the Obecní dům where the composer's *Má vlast* (*My Country*) is performed in the presence of the president, finishing on June 2 with a rendition of Beethoven's *Ninth Symphony*. Tickets for the festival sell out fast – try your luck by writing, a month before the festival begins, to the Prague Spring Festival box office at Hellichova 18, Malá Strana, ☎ 257 312 547, 🌐 www.festival.cz.

Prague International Marathon
Runners from over fifty countries come to race through the city's cobbled streets and over the Charles Bridge in late May; 🌐 www.pim.cz.

World Roma Festival (Khamoro)
International Roma festival of music, dance and film, plus seminars and workshops in late May; 🌐 www.khamoro.cz.

World Festival of Puppet Art
Week-long international puppet festival in late May/early June organized by Prague's chief puppetry institute; 🌐 www.puppetart.com.

Respect Festival
World music weekend held at various venues across the city in June, including the Akropolis and Štvanice island; 🌐 www.respectmusic.cz.

Dance Prague (Tanec Praha)
An established highlight of Prague's cultural calendar, this international festival of modern dance takes place over three weeks in June throughout the city; 🌐 www.tanecpha.cz.

Prague Autumn Festival (Pražský podzim)
Not quite as prestigious as the spring festival, but still with plenty of top-drawer performances of classical music held at the Rudolfinum in September; 🌐 www.pragueautumn.cz.

Burčák
At the end of September for a couple of weeks, temporary stalls on street corners sell the year's partially fermented new

wine, known as *burčák*, a misty, heady brew.

Christmas markets

Christmas markets selling gifts, food and mulled wine (*svářák*) are set up at several places around the city in December: the biggest ones are on Wenceslas Square and the Old Town Square. Temporary ice rinks are also constructed at various locations.

Saint Barbara

On the saint's feast day of December 4, cherry-tree branches are bought as decorations, the aim being to get them to blossom before Christmas.

Eve of St Nicholas

On the evening of December 5, numerous trios, dressed up as St Nicholas (*svatý Mikuláš*), an angel and a devil, tour round the streets, the angel handing out sweets and fruit to children who've been good,

while the devil dishes out coal and potatoes to those who've been naughty. The Czech St Nicholas has white hair and a beard, and dresses not in red but in a white priest's outfit, with a bishop's mitre.

Bohuslav Martinů Festival

Annual festival of music in early December celebrating the least well-known of the big four Czech composers; ⓦwww.martinu.cz.

Christmas Eve (Štědrý večer)

December 24 is traditionally a day of fasting, broken only when the evening star appears, signalling the beginning of the Christmas feast of carp, potato salad, schnitzel and sweetbreads. Only after the meal are the children allowed to open their presents, which miraculously appear beneath the tree, thanks not to Santa Claus, but to Baby Jesus (*Ježíšek*).

Directory

Addresses The street name is always written before the building number in Prague addresses. The city is divided into numbered postal districts: of the areas covered by the Guide, central Prague is Prague 1; southern Nové Město and half of Vinohrady is Prague 2; the rest of Vinohrady and Žižkov is Prague 3; Holešovice is Prague 7.

Banks Banking hours are Monday to Friday 8am to 5pm, often with a break at lunchtime. ATMs can be found across the city.

Bike rental City Bike, Královdorská 5 ☎776 180 274; metro Náměstí Republiky.

Car rental Czechocar, Kongresové centrum, 5 května 65, Vyšehrad ☎220 113 454, ⓦwww.czechocar.cz; Holiday Autos, Spálená 14, Nové Město ☎296 337 690, ⓦwww.holidayautos.cz.

Credit cards For lost credit cards, call the following numbers: American Express ☎222 800 222; Visa/MasterCard/Eurocard ☎272 771 111; Diners Club ☎267 197 450.

Cultural institutes Austrian Cultural Institute, Jungmannovo náměstí 18, ⓦwww.austria.cz/kultur; British Council Bredovský dvůr, Politických vězňů 13 ⓦwww.brit-

ishcouncil.cz; Goethe Institut Masarykovo nábřeží 32 ⓦwww.goethe.de/prag; Institut Français Štěpánská 35, ⓦwww.ifp.cz; Instituto Italiano di Cultura, Šporkova 14 ⓦwww.iic-praga.cz.

Dentist Palackého 5, Nové Město; metro Můstek; ☎224 946 981.

Disabled travellers The guidebook *Accessible Prague/Přístupná Praha* is available from the Prague Wheelchair Association (Pražská organizace vozíčkářů), Benediktská 6 ☎224 827 210, ⓦwww.pov.cz.

Electricity The standard continental 220 volts AC. Most European appliances should work as long as you have an adaptor for continental-style two-pin round plugs. North Americans will need this plus a transformer.

Embassies Australia, Klimentská 10, Nové Město ☎251 018 350; Britain, Thunovská 14, Malá Strana ☎257 402 111, ⓦwww.britain.cz; Canada, Muchova 6, Bubeneč ☎272 101 890, ⓦwww.canada.cz; Ireland, Tržiště 13, Malá Strana ☎257 530 061; New Zealand, Dykova 19 Vinohrady ☎222 514 672; USA Tržiště 15, Malá Strana ☎257 530 663, ⓦwww.usembassy.cz.

Emergencies ☎112; Ambulance ☎155; Police ☎158; Fire ☎150.

Exchange 24hr service, near the bottom of Wenceslas Square at 28 října 13.

Gay and lesbian Prague ⊛prague. gayguide.net.

Hospital For an English-speaking doctor, you should go to Nemocnice na Homolce, Roentgenova 2, Motol ☎257 271 111. If it's an emergency, dial ☎155 for an ambulance and you'll be taken to the nearest hospital.

Internet The following cafés have Internet access: Obecní dům (see p.101), Bohemia Bagel (see p.69), and Globe (see p.109). For details of how to get your lap-top connected when abroad, check out ⊛www. kropla.com.

Left luggage Prague's main bus and train stations have lockers and/or a 24hr left-luggage office, with instructions in English.

Lost property The main train stations have lost property offices – look for the sign ztráty a nálezy – and there's a central municipal one at Karoliny Světlé 5 (Mon–Fri only). If you've lost your passport, then get in touch with your embassy (see p.146).

Money The Czech crown or koruna česká (abbreviated to Kč or CZK) is divided into one hundred relatively worthless hellers or haléře (abbreviated to h). At the time of going to press there were around 40Kč to the pound sterling, 30Kč to the euro and around 20Kč to the US dollar. For the most up-to-date exchange rates, consult ⊛www. oanda.com or ⊛www.xe.com. Notes come in 20Kč, 50Kč, 100Kč, 200Kč, 500Kč, 1000Kč and 2000Kč (and less frequently 5000Kč) denominations; coins are 1Kč, 2Kč, 5Kč, 10Kč, 20Kč and 50Kč, plus 50h.

Newspapers You can get most foreign dailies and magazines at the kiosks at the bottom of Wenceslas Square, outside metro Můstek.

Pharmacies 24hr chemist at Palackého 5 ☎224 946 982.

Phones Most public phones take only phone cards (telefonní karty), available from post offices, tobacconists and some shops (prices vary). There are instructions in English, and if you press the appropriate button the language on the digital read-out will change to English. If you have any problems, ring ☎1181 to get through to international information.

Phone numbers Nearly all Prague phone numbers are nine digit. There is no separate city code.

Police There are two main types of police: the Policie are the national force with white shirts, navy blue jackets and grey trousers, while the Městská policie, run by the Prague city authorities, are distinguishable by their all-black uniforms. The main central police station is at Bartolomějská 6, Staré Město.

Post The main post office (pošta) is at Jindřišská 14, Nové Město ☎0800 104 4120 (daily 7am to 8pm); take a ticket and wait for your number to come up. There's a 24hr post office at Hybernská 15, Nové Město, beside Masarykovo nádraží.

Public holidays January 1, New Year's Day; Easter Monday; May 1, May Day; May 8, VE Day; July 5, Introduction of Christianity; July 6, Death of Jan Hus; September 28, Czech State Day; October 28, Foundation of the Republic; November 17, Battle for Freedom and Democracy Day; December 24, Christmas Eve; December 25, Christmas Day; December 26, St Stephen's Day.

Time The Czech Republic is on Central European Time (CET), one hour ahead of Britain and six hours ahead of EST, with the clocks going forward in spring and back again some time in autumn – the exact date changes from year to year. Generally speaking, Czechs use the 24-hour clock.

Toilets Apart from the automatic ones in central Prague, public toilets (záchody, toalety or WC) are few and far between. In some, you have to buy toilet paper (by the sheet) from the attendant, whom you will also have to pay as you enter. Standards of hygiene can be low. Gentlemen should head for muži or páni; ladies should head for ženy or dámy.

Chronology

Chronology

895 ▶ First recorded Přemyslid duke and first Christian ruler of Prague, Bořivoj, baptized by saints Cyril and Methodius.

929 ▶ Prince Václav (better known as Good King Wenceslas) is martyred by his pagan brother Boleslav the Cruel.

1212 ▶ Otakar I secures a royal title for himself and his descendants, who thereafter become King of Bohemia.

1305 ▶ Václav II dies heirless and the Přemyslid dynasty comes to an end.

1346–78 ▶ During the reign of Holy Roman Emperor Charles IV, Prague enjoys its first Golden Age as the city is transformed by building projects into a fitting imperial capital.

1415 ▶ Czech religious reformer, Jan Hus, is found guilty of heresy and burnt at the stake in Konstanz (Constance).

1419 ▶ Prague's first defenestration. Hus's followers, known as the Hussites, throw several councillors (including the mayor) to their deaths from the windows of Prague's Nové Město's town hall.

1420 ▶ Battle of Vítkov (a hill in Prague). Jan Žižka leads the Hussites to victory over the papal forces.

1434 ▶ Battle of Lipany. The radical Hussites are defeated by an army of moderates and Catholics.

1526 ▶ The beginning of Habsburg (and Catholic) rule in Prague, as Emperor Ferdinand I is elected King of Bohemia.

1576–1611 ▶ Emperor Rudolf II establishes Prague as the royal seat of power, and ushers in the city's second Golden Age, summoning artists, astronomers and alchemists from all over Europe.

1618 ▶ Prague's second defenestration. Two Catholic governors are thrown from the windows of Prague Castle by Bohemian Protestants. The Thirty Years' War begins.

1620 ▶ Battle of the White Mountain, just outside Prague. The Protestants, under the "Winter King" Frederick of the Palatinate, are defeated by the Catholic forces; 27 Protestant nobles are executed on Old Town Square.

1648 ▶ The (Protestant) Swedes are defeated on Charles Bridge by Prague's Jewish and student populations. The Thirty Years' War ends.

1781 ▶ Edict of Tolerance issued by Emperor Joseph II, allowing a large degree of freedom of worship for the first time in 150 years.

1848 ▶ Uprising in Prague eventually put down by Habsburg commander Alfred Prince Windischgätz. The ensuing reforms allow Jews to settle outside the ghetto for the first time.

1918 ▶ The Habsburg Empire collapses due to defeat in World War I. Czechoslovakia founded.

1938 ▶ According to the Munich Agreement drawn up by Britain, France, Fascist Italy and Nazi Germany, the Czechs are forced to secede the border regions of the Sudetenland to Hitler.

1939 ▶ The Germans invade and occupy the rest of the Czech Lands. Slovakia declares independence.

1941 ▶ Prague's Jews deported to Terezín (Theresienstadt) before being sent to the camps.

1942 ▶ Nazi leader Reinhardt Heydrich assassinated in Prague. The villages of Lidice and Ležáky are annihilated in retaliation.

1945 ▶ On May 5, the Prague Uprising against the Nazis begins. On May 9, the Russians liberate the city. The city's ethnic German population is brutally expelled.

1946 ▶ Communist Party wins up to forty percent of the vote in first postwar general election.

1948 ▶ Communist Party seizes power in a bloodless coup. Thousands flee the country.

1952 ▶ Twelve leading Party members (eleven of them Jewish) sentenced to death as traitors in Prague's infamous Stalinist show trials.

1968 ▶ During the "Prague Spring", reformers within the Party abolish censorship. Soviet troops invade the country and put a stop to the reform movement. Thousands go into exile.

1977 ▶ 243 Czechs and Slovaks, including playwright Václav Havel, sign Charter 77 manifesto, kickstarting the dissident movement.

1989 ▶ After two weeks of popular protest, known as the Velvet Revolution, the Communist government resigns. Havel is elected as president.

1993 ▶ Czechoslovakia splits into the Czech Republic and Slovakia.

2004 ▶ The Czech Republic enters the European Union.

Language

Czech

A modicum of English is spoken in Prague's central restaurants and hotels, and among the city's younger generation. Any attempt to speak Czech will be heartily appreciated, though don't be discouraged if people seem not to understand, as most will be unaccustomed to hearing foreigners stumble through their language. Unfortunately, Czech (český) is a highly complex western Slav tongue, into which you're unlikely to make much headway during a short stay.

Pronunciation

English-speakers often find Czech impossibly difficult to pronounce: just try the Czech tongue-twister, strč prst skrz krk (stick your finger down your neck). The good news is that, apart from a few special letters, each letter and syllable is pronounced as it's written – the trick is always to stress the first syllable of a word, no matter what its length; otherwise you'll render it unintelligible.

Short and long vowels

Czech has both short and long vowels (the latter being denoted by a variety of accents):

a like the u in cup
á as in father
e as in pet
é as in fair
ě like the ye in yes
i or y as in pit
í or ý as in seat
o as in not
ó as in door
u like the oo in book
ů or ú like the oo in fool

Vowel combinations and diphthongs

There are very few diphthongs in Czech, so any combinations of vowels other than those below should be pronounced as two separate syllables.

au like the ou in foul
ou like the oe in foe

Consonants and accents

There are no silent consonants, but it's worth remembering that r and l can form a syllable if standing between two other consonants or at the end of a word, as in Brno (Br-no) or Vltava (Vl-ta-va). The consonants listed below are those which differ substantially from the English. Accents look daunting, particularly the háček, which appears above c, d, l, n, r, s, t and z, but the only one

The alphabet

In the Czech alphabet, letters which feature a háček (as in the č of the word itself) are considered separate letters and appear in Czech indexes immediately after their more familiar cousins. More confusingly, the consonant combination ch is also considered as a separate letter and appears in Czech indexes after the letter h.

which causes a lot of problems is ř, probably the most difficult letter to say in the entire language – even Czech toddlers have to be taught how to say it.

c like the **ts** in boats
č like the **ch** in chicken
ch like the **ch** in the Scottish loch
d' like the **d** in duped
g always as in goat, never as in general
h always as in have, but more energetic
j like the **y** in yoke

kd pronounced as **gd**
l' like the **lli** in colliery
mě pronounced as mnye
ň like the **n** in nuance
p softer than the English **p**
r as in rip, but often rolled
ř like the sound of **r** and **ž** combined
š like the **sh** in shop
ť like the **t** in tutor
ž like the **s** in pleasure; at the end of a
word like the **sh** in shop

Words and phrases

Basics

Yes	ano
No	ne
Please/excuse me	prosím vás
Don't mention it	není zač
Sorry	pardon
Thank you	děkuju
Bon appétit	dobrou chuť
Bon voyage	šťstnou cestu
Hello/goodbye (informal)	ahoj
Hello (formal)	dobrý den
Goodbye (formal)	na shledanou
Good morning	dobré ráno
Good evening	dobrý večer
Good night (when leaving)	dobrou noc
How are you?	jak se máte?
I'm	ja jsem
English	angličan(ka)
Irish/Scottish	ir(ka)/skot(ka)/
Welsh	velšan(ka)/
American	američan(ka)
Do you speak English?	mluvíte anglicky?
I don't speak German	nemluvím německy
I don't understand	nerozumím
I understand	rozumím
I don't know	nevím
Speak slowly	mluvíte pomalu
How do you say that in Czech?	jak se tohle řekne česky?
Could you write it down for me?	mužete mí to napsat?
Today	dnes
Yesterday	včera
Tomorrow	zítra

The day after tomorrow	pozítří
Now	hnet
Later	později
Wait a minute!	moment
Leave me alone!	dej mi pokoj!
Go away!	jdi pryč!
Help!	pomoc!
This one	tento
A little	trochu
Another one	ještě jedno -
Large/small	velký/malý
More/less	více/méně
Good/bad	dobrý/špatný
Cheap/expensive	levný/drahý
Hot/cold	horký/studený
With/without	s/bez
The bill please	zaplatím prosím
Do you have …?	máte …?
We don't have	nemáme
We do have	máme

Questions

What?	co?
Where?	kde?
When?	kdy?
Why?	proč?
Which one?	který/ktera?
This one?	ten/ta?
How many?	kolík?
What time does it open?	kdy máte otevřeno?
What time does it close?	kdy zavíráte?

Getting around

Over here	tady
Over there	tam

Left	nalevo
Right	napravo
Straight on	rovně
Where is …?	kde je …?
How do I get to Prague?	jak se dostanu do Prahy ?
How do I get to the…?	jak se dostanu k …?
By bus	autobusem
By train	vlakem
By car	autem
On foot	pěšky
By taxi	taxíkem
Stop here, please	zastavte tady, prosím
Ticket	jízdenka/lístek
Return ticket	zpáteční
Railway station	nádraží
Bus station	autobusové nádraží
Bus stop	autobusová zastávka
When's the next train to Prague?	kdy jede další vlak do Prahy?
Is it going to Prague?	jede to do Prahy?
Do I have to change?	musím přestupovat?
Do I need a reservation?	musím mít místenku?
Is this seat free?	je tu volna?
May we (sit down)?	můžeme (se sednout)?

Accommodation

Are there any rooms available?	máte volné pokoje?
Do you have a double room?	máte jednou dvou lůžkovy pokoj?
For one night	na jednu noc
With shower	se sprchou
With bath	s koupelnou
How much is it?	kolík to stojí?
With breakfast?	se snídaně?

Some signs

Entrance	vchod
Exit	východ
Toilets	záchody/toalety
Men	muži
Women	ženy
Ladies	dámy
Gentlemen	pánové
Open	otevřeno
Closed	zavřeno
Pull/Push	sem/tam
Danger!	pozor!
Hospital	nemocnice

No smoking	kouření zakázáno
No entry	vstup zakázán
Arrival	příjezd
Departure	odjezd

Days of the week

Monday	pondělí
Tuesday	uterý
Wednesday	středa
Thursday	čtvrtek
Friday	pátek
Saturday	sobota
Sunday	neděle
Day	den
Week	týden
Month	měsíc
Year	rok

Months of the year

Many Slav languages have their own highly individual systems in which the words for the names of the months are descriptive nouns, sometimes beautifully apt for the month in question.

January	leden (ice)
February	únor (hibernation)
March	březen (birch)
April	duben (oak)
May	květen (blossom)
June	červen (red)
July	červenec (redder)
August	srpen (sickle)
September	zaří (blazing)
October	říjen (rutting)
November	listopad (leaves falling)
December	prosinec (slaughter of pigs)

Numbers

1	jeden
2	dva
3	tří
4	čtyři
5	pět
6	šest
7	sedm
8	osm
9	devět
10	deset
11	jedenáct
12	dvanáct
13	třináct

14	čtrnáct	90	devadesát
15	patnáct	100	sto
16	šestnáct	101	sto jedna
17	sedmnáct	155	sto padesát pět
18	osmnáct	200	dvě stě
19	devatenáct	300	tři sta
20	dvacet	400	čtyři sta
21	dvacetjedna	500	pět set
30	třicet	600	šest set
40	čtyřicet	700	sedm set
50	padesát	800	osm set
60	šedesát	900	devět set
70	sedmdesát	1000	tisíc
80	osmdesát		

Food and drink terms

Basics

chléb	bread
chlebíček	(open) sandwich
cukr	sugar
hořčice	mustard
houska	round roll
knedlíky	dumplings
křen	horseradish
lžíce	spoon
maso	meat
máslo	butter
med	honey
mléko	milk
moučník	dessert
nápoje	drinks
na zdraví	cheers!
nůž	knife
oběd	lunch
obloha	garnish
ocet	vinegar
ovoce	fruit
pečivo	pastry
pepř	pepper
polévka	soup
předkrmy	starters
přílohy	side dishes
rohlík	finger roll
rybby	fish
rýže	rice
sklenice	glass
snídaně	breakfast
sůl	salt
šálek	cup
talíř	plate
tartarská omáčka	tartare sauce
večeře	supper/dinner
vejce	eggs
vidlička	fork
volské oko	fried egg
zeleniny	vegetables

Common terms

čerstvý	fresh
domácí	home-made
dušený	stew/casserole
grilovaný	roast on the spit
kyselý	sour
na kmíně	with caraway seeds
na roštu	grilled
nadívaný	stuffed
nakládaný	pickled
(za)pečený	baked/roast
plněný	stuffed
s.m. (s máslem)	with butter
sladký	sweet
slaný	salted
smažený	fried in breadcrumbs
studený	cold
syrový	raw
sýrový	cheesy
teplý	hot
uzený	smoked
vařený	boiled
znojmský	with gherkins

Soups

boršč	beetroot soup
bramborová	potato soup
čočková	lentil soup
fazolová	bean soup

hovězí vývar	beef broth
hrachová	pea soup
kapustnica	sauerkraut, mushroom and meat soup
kuřecí	thin chicken soup
rajská	tomato soup
zeleninová	vegetable soup

Fish

kapr	carp
losos	salmon
makrela	mackerel
platýs	flounder
pstruh	trout
rybí filé	fillet of fish
sardinka	sardine
štika	pike
treska	cod
zavináč	herring/rollmop

Meat dishes

bažant	pheasant
biftek	beef steak
čevapčiči	spicy meat balls
dršťky	tripe
drůbež	poultry
guláš	goulash
hovězí	beef
husa	goose
játra	liver
jazyk	tongue
kachna	duck
klobásy	sausages
kotleta	cutlet
kuře	chicken
kýta	leg
ledvinky	kidneys
řízek	steak
roštěná	sirloin
salám	salami
sekaná	meat loaf
skopové maso	mutton
slanina	bacon
svíčková	fillet of beef
šunka	ham
telecí	veal
vepřový	pork
vepřové řízek	breaded pork cutlet or schnitzel
zajíc	hare
žebírko	ribs

Vegetables

brambory	potatoes
brokolice	broccoli
celer	celery
cibule	onion
česnek	garlic
chřest	asparagus
čočka	lentils
fazole	beans
houby	mushrooms
hranolky	chips, French fries
hrášek	peas
karot	carrot
květák	cauliflower
kyselá okurka	pickled gherkin
kyselé zelí	sauerkraut
lečo	ratatouille
lilek	aubergine
okurka	cucumber
pórek	leek
rajče	tomato
ředkev	radish
řepná bulva	beetroot
špenát	spinach
zelí	cabbage
žampiony	mushrooms

Fruit, cheese and nuts

banán	banana
borůvky	blueberries
broskev	peach
brusinky	cranberries
bryndza	goat's cheese in brine
citrón	lemon
grejp	grapefruit
hermelín	Czech brie
hrozny	grapes
hruška	pear
jablko	apple
jahody	strawberries
kompot	stewed fruit
maliny	raspberries
mandle	almonds
meruňka	apricot
niva	semi-soft, crumbly, blue cheese
oříšky	peanuts
ostružiny	blackberries
oštěpek	heavily smoked, curd cheese
parenica	rolled strips of lightly smoked, curd cheese

pivní sýr	cheese flavoured with beer
pomeranč	orange
rozinky	raisins
švestky	plums
třešně	cherries
tvaroh	fresh curd cheese
urda	soft, fresh, whey cheese
uzený sýr	smoked cheese
vlašské ořechy	walnuts

Drinks

čaj	tea
destiláty	spirits
káva	coffee
koňak	brandy
láhev	bottle
minerální (voda)	mineral (water)
mléko	milk
pivo	beer
presso	espresso
s ledem	with ice
soda	soda
suché víno	dry wine
šumivý	fizzy
svařené víno /svařák	mulled wine
tonic	tonic
vinný střik	white wine with soda
víno	wine

Travel store

Egypt
Gambia
Jordan
Kenya
Marrakesh **D**
Morocco
South Africa,
  Lesotho &
  Swaziland
Syria
Tanzania
Tunisia
West Africa
Zanzibar

Travel Specials
First-Time Africa
First-Time
  Around the
  World
First-Time Asia
First-Time
  Europe
First-Time Latin
  America
Travel Health
Travel Online
Travel Survival
Walks in London
  & SE England
Women Travel
World Party

Maps
Algarve
Amsterdam
Andalucia
  & Costa del Sol
Argentina
Athens
Australia
Barcelona
Berlin
Boston &
  Cambridge
Brittany
Brussels
California
Chicago
Chile
Corsica
Costa Rica
  & Panama
Crete
Croatia
Cuba
Cyprus
Czech Republic
Dominican
  Republic
Dubai & UAE

Dublin
Egypt
Florence & Siena
Florida
France
Frankfurt
Germany
Greece
Guatemala &
  Belize
Iceland
India
Ireland
Italy
Kenya &
  Northern
  Tanzania
Lisbon
London
Los Angeles
Madrid
Malaysia
Mallorca
Marrakesh
Mexico
Miami & Key
  West
Morocco
New England
New York City
New Zealand
Northern Spain
Paris
Peru
Portugal
Prague
Pyrenees &
  Andorra
Rome
San Francisco
Sicily
South Africa
South India
Spain & Portugal
Sri Lanka
Tenerife
Thailand
Toronto
Trinidad &
  Tobago
Tunisia
Turkey
Tuscany
Venice
Vietnam, Laos
  & Cambodia
Washington DC
Yucatán
  Peninsula

Dictionary
Phrasebooks
Croatian
Czech
Dutch
Egyptian Arabic
French
German
Greek
Hindi & Urdu
Italian
Japanese
Latin American
  Spanish
Mandarin
  Chinese
Mexican Spanish
Polish
Portuguese
Russian
Spanish
Swahili
Thai
Turkish
Vietnamese

Computers
Blogging
eBay
iPhone
iPods, iTunes
  & music online
The Internet
Macs & OS X
MySpace
PCs and Windows
PlayStation
  Portable
Website Directory

Film & TV
American
  Independent
  Film
British Cult
  Comedy
Chick Flicks
Comedy Movies
Cult Movies
Film
Film Musicals
Film Noir
Gangster Movies
Horror Movies
Kids' Movies
Sci-Fi Movies
Westerns

Lifestyle
Babies

Ethical Living
Pregnancy
  & Birth
Running

Music Guides
The Beatles
Blues
Bob Dylan
Book of Playlists
Classical Music
Elvis
Frank Sinatra
Heavy Metal
Hip-Hop
Jazz
Led Zeppelin
Opera
Pink Floyd
Punk
Reggae
Rock
The Rolling
  Stones
Soul and R&B
Velvet
  Underground
World Music
  (2 vols)

Popular Culture
Books for
  Teenagers
Children's Books,
  5-11
Conspiracy
  Theories
Crime Fiction
Cult Fiction
The Da Vinci
  Code
His Dark
  Materials
Lord of the Rings
Shakespeare
Superheroes
The Templars
Unexplained
  Phenomena

Science
The Brain
Climate Change
The Earth
Genes & Cloning
The Universe
Weather

For more information go to www.roughguides.com

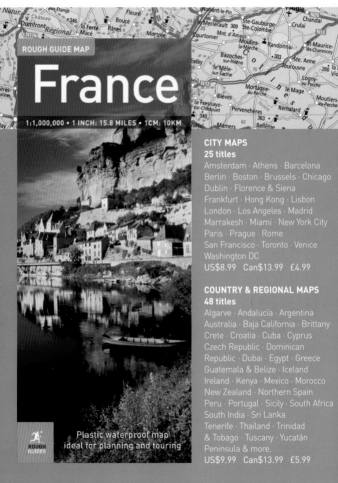

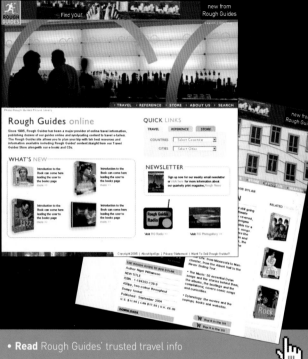

Listen Up!

"You may be used to the Rough Guide series being comprehensive, but nothing will prepare you for the exhaustive Rough Guide to World Music . . . one of our books of the year."

Sunday Times, London

Rough Guide Music Titles

The Beatles • Blues • Bob Dylan • Classical Music Elvis • Frank Sinatra • Heavy Metal • Hip-Hop iPods, iTunes & music online • Jazz • Book of Playlists Led Zeppelin • Opera • Pink Floyd • Punk • Reggae Rock • The Rolling Stones • Soul and R&B • World Music Vol 1 & 2 • Velvet Underground

NOTES

small print & Index

SMALL PRINT

A Rough Guide to Rough Guides

In 1981, Mark Ellingham, a recent graduate in English from Bristol University, was travelling in Greece on a tiny budget and couldn't find the right guidebook. With a group of friends he wrote his own guide, combining a contemporary, journalistic style with a practical approach to travellers' needs. That first Rough Guide was a student scheme that became a publishing phenomenon. Today, Rough Guides include recommendations from shoestring to luxury and cover hundreds of destinations around the globe, including almost every country in the Americas and Europe, more than half of Africa and most of Asia and Australasia. Millions of readers relish Rough Guides' wit and inquisitiveness as much as their enthusiastic, critical approach and value-for-money ethos. The guides' ever-growing team of authors and photographers is spread all over the world.

In the early 1990s, Rough Guides branched out of travel, with the publication of Rough Guides to World Music, Classical Music and the Internet. All three have become benchmark titles in their fields, spearheading the publication of a range of more than 350 titles under the Rough Guide name, including phrasebooks, waterproof maps, music guides from Opera to Heavy Metal, reference works as diverse as Conspiracy Theories and Shakespeare, and popular culture books from iPods to Poker. Rough Guides also produce a series of more than 120 World Music CDs in partnership with World Music Network.

Visit www.roughguides.com to see our latest publications.

Rough Guide travel images are available for commercial licensing at www.roughguidespictures.com

Publishing information

This 2nd edition published May 2008 by
Rough Guides Ltd, 80 Strand, London WC2R 0RL.
345 Hudson St, 4th Floor, New York, NY 10014,
USA.

Distributed by the Penguin Group
Penguin Books Ltd, 80 Strand, London WC2R 0RL
Penguin Group (USA), 375 Hudson Street, NY
10014, USA
14 Local Shopping Centre, Panchsheel Park, New
Delhi 110017, India
Penguin Group (Australia), 250 Camberwell Road,
Camberwell, Victoria 3124, Australia
Penguin Group (Canada), 10 Alcorn Avenue,
Toronto, ON M4V 1E4, Canada
Penguin Group (NZ), 67 Apollo Drive, Mairangi Bay,
Auckland 1310, New Zealand
Typeset in Bembo and Helvetica to an original
design by Henry Iles.

Cover concept by Peter Dyer.

Printed and bound in China
© Rob Humphreys 2008

A catalogue record for this book is available from
the British Library

ISBN 978-1-85828-282-4

The publishers and authors have done their best
to ensure the accuracy and currency of all the
information in Prague DIRECTIONS, however, they
can accept no responsibility for any loss, injury, or
inconvenience sustained by any traveller as a result
of information or advice contained in the guide.

1   3   5   7   9   8   6   4   2

Help us update

We've gone to a lot of effort to ensure that the second edition of Prague DIRECTIONS is accurate and up-to-date. However, things change – places get "discovered", opening hours are notoriously fickle, restaurants and rooms raise prices or lower standards. If you feel we've got it wrong or left something out, we'd like to know, and if you can remember the address, the price, the phone number, so much the better.

Please send your comments with the subject line "Prague DIRECTIONS Update" to ©mail@roughguides.com. We'll credit all contributions and send a copy of the next edition (or any other Rough Guide if you prefer) for the very best emails.

Have your questions answered and tell others about your trip at ⊛community.roughguides.com

Rough Guide credits

Text editor: Gavin Thomas
Layout: Dan May
Photography: Jon Cunningham
Cartography: Jai Prakesh Mishra

Picture editor: Sarah Cummins
Proofreader: Jan McCann
Production: Rebecca Short
Cover design: Chloë Roberts

SMALL PRINT

The author

Rob Humphreys has travelled extensively in central and eastern Europe, writing guides to Prague, the Czech and Slovak Republics, and St Petersburg, as well as London and Scotland.

Photo credits

All images © Rough Guides except the following:

Front cover picture: Tourists by Pyramid, Louvre, Paris © John Lamb/Getty
Front bottom image: Trevi fountain, Rome © 4Corners/Amantini Stefano
Back cover picture: Plaça Reial, Barcelona © Rough Guides
p.1 Old Town cafés © Photolibrary
p.2 Charles Bridge © Photolibrary
p.3 Street sign © Photolibrary
p.4 Malá Strana © Photolibrary

p.6 Guard at Prague Castle © Alamy
p.7 Prague Castle © Photolibrary
p.7 Old Town Square © Photolibrary
p.11 Charles Bridge © Photolibrary
p.11 Wenceslas Square © axiom/DK
p.22 Mucha poster © Corbis
p.38 Museum of Communism poster © Alistair Laming/Alamy
p.39 Memorial to the Victims of Communism © Stephen Saks Photography/Alamy

Index

Maps are marked in colour

INDEX